MEET THE
CANDIDATES
2020

ELIZABETH
WARREN

ELIZABETH WARREN

A VOTER'S GUIDE

Series Edited by
SCOTT DWORKIN

Compiled and Written by Grant Stern

Skyhorse Publishing

Skyhorse Publishing books may be purchased in bulk at special discounts for sales promotion, corporate gifts, fund-raising, or educational purposes. Special editions can also be created to specifications. For details, contact the Special Sales Department, Skyhorse Publishing, 307 West 36th Street, 11th Floor, New York, NY 10018 or info@skyhorsepublishing.com.

Skyhorse® and Skyhorse Publishing® are registered trademarks of Skyhorse Publishing, Inc.®, a Delaware corporation.

Visit our website at www.skyhorsepublishing.com.

10 9 8 7 6 5 4 3 2 1

Library of Congress Cataloging-in-Publication Data is available on file.

Cover design by Brian Peterson
Cover photo credit: Office of Senator Elizabeth Warren

ISBN: 978-1-5107-5024-1
Ebook ISBN: 978-1-5107-5032-6

Printed in the United States of America

CONTENTS

ELIZABETH WARREN

INTRODUCTION TO ELIZABETH WARREN

BY SERIES EDITOR SCOTT DWORKIN

The first time I met Elizabeth Warren was in November 2012 during her victory party at a friend's DC office, celebrating her defeat of Senator Scott Brown (R-MA). The event was supposed to be an informal meet and greet, hosted by some of the advisers who worked on her campaign. Just a few people getting together. I arrived at the office and it was packed; she was there. After catching up with friends, I slowly but surely made my way toward the senator-elect. I was about to introduce myself, but at that moment it was time for her to give some remarks. When she finished talking to the room, we immediately said hello to each other.

She and I spent a minute or so talking, but not about politics. It was about my T-shirt, which was the image of the cover of the book *Animal Farm*. It wasn't about if I was a donor, if I could raise her money, throw an event, if I represented a political action committee or any of the numerous things typical politicians want to know in DC. It was about my T-shirt and Orwell's book. Having a conversation with her isn't like speaking to most other politicians.

My first impression of Senator-elect Warren after meeting her, and after that campaign, was that she was fearless. She wasn't going to be intimidated by anyone, including big banks or folks on Wall Street. She wasn't going to be deterred from taking hard stances against gigantic corporations that were abusing the American people. And that stance wouldn't change just because you gave her money.

My first impression was right.

I thought to myself, this is how true progressives operate. This is the beginning of a true progressive leader joining the Senate. Someone who cannot be bought.

Warren became that progressive leader because she took a chance and decided to run against a Republican incumbent in Massachusetts. It took what felt like forever for her to decide to run, not just to build suspense, but to actually take the time to think about it. It definitely looked like an uphill climb, so one could understand hesitation. The Harvard professor wound up pummeling Senator Brown by more than seven points. She overperformed in nearly nine out of the ten polls in the race.

Now, Elizabeth Warren is taking that same grit and bringing it to the national stage in her run for president. You could tell the moment she announced that her candidacy would be taken very seriously. She was immediately perceived as a viable challenger by President Trump and his political allies. Trump had attacked Warren over her family's oral history of Native American ancestry by assigning her the racist nickname of "Pocahontas." He continued those unpresidential attacks the day she announced her candidacy. On February 9, 2019, the day Warren launched her campaign, the President tweeted, "Today Elizabeth Warren, sometimes referred to by me as Pocahontas, joined the race for President. Will she run as our first Native American presidential candidate, or has she decided that after 32 years, this is not playing so well anymore? See you on the campaign TRAIL, Liz!"

It was his eighth tweet attacking Senator Warren in the last two years.

Trump was obviously attacking Warren because she is a clear threat to his presidency, both in the Senate and in her bid for the White House. He doesn't want people to realize that you can actually have a thought-provoking and inspirational person like Senator Warren in the White House. Ironically, voters have shown with a remarkable consistency that they're uninterested in her family's oral history, just as polling has shown since her first Senate race. It's only a matter of interest to journalists.

It takes a lot of guts to step up and take on corruption at the highest levels, which Senator Warren has made the top issue of her campaign. It's not easy. And that's exactly what Warren's done in her time in the Senate since day one. Things have—obviously—been kicked up a notch corruption-wise in this country as of late. Warren's leadership fighting against those who defraud the American people is needed now more than ever. And Warren has been more than up for the challenge.

To make it clear her campaign wouldn't be influenced by donors, Senator Warren made a bold move with her 2020 presidential campaign to not hold any high-dollar fund-raisers, or focus on fund-raising on the phones like most candidates. As a person who had to direct hundreds of candidates to fund-raise over the course of the last decade, it was pretty refreshing to hear someone commit to changing the status quo for how a presidential campaign operates. Fund-raising calls take up a lot of time and energy. Many political candidates, including incumbents, are forced to make well over eight hours of calls for money per day. At the minimum.

Most first-time candidates for political office would love to be able to make the pledge of making no donor calls, but they aren't able to have an operational campaign without money. Due to Warren's massive groundswell of grassroots support, she doesn't have to rely on gigantic donors or independent expenditure groups like super PACs to support her campaign.

Instead, she can focus on voters and championing their needs.

But of course, her pledge to not really have a full-fledged fund-raising operation also has its pitfalls. The more money you have, the more staff you can hire, the more ads you can run, and so on. And with such a crowded field, money may be one of the determining factors of viability when considering who to vote for in the Democratic primary. In the end, I think her decision to leave big money out of her own politics now is well worth the risk.

If you want to truly flush out corruption in politics, you're going to have to take bold steps to make it clear that you can't be bought. Not having a traditional fund-raising operation should rid people of most doubt.

Senator Warren can't pass a constitutional amendment to overturn the *Citizens United* court decision, but she's going to hold her own campaign accountable.

Rebuilding America's middle class has become a major issue being pushed by Warren's campaign. Warren wants people to be able to live a comfortable life, not have to struggle constantly, or stress about having enough money to keep the lights on.

Nobody should worry *if* they're going put food on their tables. Nobody working a full-time job should worry about earning a livable wage or the cost of health insurance. They shouldn't have to work multiple jobs just to make ends meet. And sometimes that's not even enough. As it stands, most Americans don't even have enough money to cover a $1,000 emergency. People are struggling just to get by.

Warren was the fortunate beneficiary of having a family member available to help raise her two children. That's why she believes nobody with kids should have to pray for good fortune just to find affordable child care for babies and toddlers.

Warren believes everyone should get a fair shake, and doesn't believe the US government is doing enough to make it happen. Given the tough financial position a lot of Americans are in, it's fair to say there needs to be a fighter in the White House who can help people get back on their feet.

She has real plans with real independent analysis that would lower the cost of rent across America, create jobs, provide a universal child care plan, and raise taxes on the very wealthiest few to end loopholes that the ultra-wealthy use to evade paying their fair share. These are commonsense reforms that will be complex to overhaul, which is Warren's specialty. She knows how to assemble vast amounts of data and figure out what really works and has the skills to direct a team to make that happen.

In order to rebuild the middle class, we need a president who understands the people, not one who grew up on a silver spoon.

We need a president who has compassion, empathy, and love, things that are wrongfully missing from politics nowadays. But these are characteristics Warren has always displayed during her tenure in the Senate.

Warren cares about people. She cares about stopping the abuse of people. She cares when regular people are being taken advantage of by predatory businesses and financial institutions. And she's smart enough to come up with the route to dig our way out of it to make it so that the consumer is protected, so the American people are protected under the law. Not just rich people.

Only a progressive fighter like her, or a fighter in general, would be able to take on some of the richest, most powerful people in the world head-on. And she has. America deserves a leader like Warren in the Oval Office, one who isn't afraid to fight. Who's not afraid to push as hard as they can against corruption and fraud. America needs a leader who doesn't base their legislative decisions on whether or not someone will contribute to their next fund-raising event, or help raise funds from their friends.

Most elected officials would be cautious in their questioning at committee hearings, because they wouldn't want to make a large potential contributor angry. Warren just wants what's best for most of Americans, which makes it much easier for her to stand up for them. She isn't worried about whether or not someone will host a fund-raiser in New York City or Los Angeles. She isn't super careful about what she says with the fear that if she says something bad about a company, they won't support her reelection bid. No, she does what she thinks is right. And it's not based on the money. So when it comes to saving the middle class, I think Warren would be one of the best fits to do it. She can take complex legislation and translate it so the American people can understand how it benefits them. Just like she did for her students at Harvard, translating complex issues so they could learn and grow. Just like she did in her congressional testimony. Just like she did with her many books, one of which landed on the *New York Times* Best Sellers List.

Warren's also got the sort of leadership style where she can take complex types of fraud (intentionally complex only so the fraudsters can take advantage of people) and simplify it so people can understand the fraud and try to avoid it in the future. Then you can update the laws to ensure that if that fraud happened again, people would end up in prison for it. Warren obviously isn't running because she is power hungry. She's running to make a difference in every American's life.

Her campaign is centered around the American people and how she can make life easier for them. She wouldn't be making money on the side. There would be no frequent weekend golf retreats to a resort she owned. She'd be focused on working, as the President of the United States. We wouldn't even have to be afraid of her using Twitter, or the presidency in general, as a weapon.

Another major part of Warren's appeal is her focus on protecting Americans. Should every person have to have to be as knowledgeable as a lawyer to use this country's financial system? Senator Warren's policy approach brings commonsense solutions to financial disclosures to make sure that everyone knows what they're getting before they sign on the dotted line.

Her ideas regarding these issues are great, because she approaches it from a 360-degree viewpoint. She doesn't just look at the dangers all Americans face from one policy talking point, or a catchphrase, like Trump's wall.

What you can expect is that Elizabeth Warren will find a position that is practical and never stop working until it becomes a reality.

When it comes to protecting Americans, it needs to be a comprehensive plan like the one Warren outlines for her campaign. We need to protect Americans not just from security threats, but also from those who threaten people financially and the threat people face of not being able to afford quality health care. It also needs to address the harm financial institutions have caused the American people. And needs to focus on making sure we don't face more election interference from foreign adversaries like Russia.

Her leadership would be great in regards to protecting Americans. Now, do I think that she can win? Absolutely. I think that when people begin to learn more about Senator Warren, they'll realize what a pragmatic candidate she is and come to understand that America needs a leader like her right now in the White House. Our country needs a president who cares about making sure that there isn't any fine print that takes advantage of the typical American; that there isn't some kind of magical footnote that makes you a pawn in the game of a large financial institution. Our country needs a president who cares about the American people in general. Right now, the bar is low. Too low.

Everything the Warren for President campaign is doing thus far is well thought out and methodical, similar to Barack Obama's campaign in 2008. And I don't expect that to change. Warren has assembled an experienced team of trusted campaign professionals. She seems to have hired good people who know the ropes and will be able to bring a formidable challenge to every other candidate in the race. One takeaway readers might have from this book is being surprised to learn just how much Warren and her ideas influenced President Obama.

A presidential nominee needs to know how to influence the national political conversation. Warren has been doing it for more than the last decade.

And something else that sets Senator Warren apart from the field is the fact she is battle-tested and ready to combat a lot of the newer challenges candidates haven't yet faced. Obama didn't face as much early scrutiny as she already has from the sitting president during his primary; it's something that in some ways hurts and in other ways helps her candidacy. While she didn't get a bestselling book out of being attacked by Trump, it has raised her national profile immeasurably.

Most of the other Democratic candidates haven't been attacked by the sitting president on his Twitter feed, during press conferences, and every chance Trump can slip a jab in. Don't expect Warren to take it sitting down. She never has, and she never will. As time progresses on the campaign trail, rest assured she will strike back with more provocative and frequent rebuttals to Trump.

Heck, she has even released her tax returns already during her Senate race,[1] even though it's not required. There aren't many known unknowns about Warren. That's also where she sharpened her message about the damage Republicans want to do to this country along with Donald Trump, telling her opponent this during a debate, according to Boston.com:

> *Let's talk about, if we're going to talk about character, what it means to have Donald Trump's back. It means, of*

course, being the vote to roll back health care for tens of millions of Americans.

It means a trillion-and-a-half-dollar tax giveaway, and paid for, the Republicans say, by cutting Social Security and Medicare. It means standing by Donald Trump when he calls white supremacists in Charlottesville fine people.

In regards to campaign strategy, Warren will likely become less focused on Iowa, and more focused on a couple of states down the line from early in the race. And of course, she will become less focused on attacking Trump. But she will be mostly focused on what she has to offer to the American people, which is considerable.

The Democratic primary in 2020 is obviously going to be a tough hill to climb for every candidate, because there are so many other parties in the race. And Warren does have some baggage from being the target of racist comments coming from Donald Trump. But I don't think that that's going to outweigh her positives, which we will elaborate upon in detail in the chapters to come.

Her vision for the future is bright, and Senator Warren's road map to winning the nomination will heavily rest on what happens in the debates, and eventually results in the early primary states. She was a champion debater in Oklahoma.

If she were president, the people of America would benefit the most. That's a fact. We would be lucky to have someone so respectful of the Constitution, of our laws and institutions, someone who is honest and diplomatic, back in the White House. Someone who actually cares about the American people, not just the uber rich and the corporations. Someone who has the strength and the heart to clean up the mess that's been left. Someone who can make our country great again.

The bottom line is that Senator Warren can beat President Trump in a head-to-head contest.

America would be lucky to have her in the White House.

She would make a great president.

WHAT DEFINES WARREN

Senator Elizabeth Warren became the first high-profile Democratic candidate to declare their candidacy for president. On New Year's Eve 2018, Senator Warren moved forward with an audacious campaign plan to save capitalism from itself. It's exactly kind of plan the former Harvard Law professor has spent the last thirty years studying, writing about, and ultimately running for Congress to pursue, before becoming the senior senator from Massachusetts less than a month after she was sworn in, when Senator John Kerry resigned to serve as Secretary of State in the second term of the Obama administration.

But Senator Warren's candidacy brings with it more than just legal experience. Her font of financial knowledge is born of years' worth of deep research into the economic lives of middle-class Americans and their ever-increasing trips through bankruptcy. Her economic focus has led her to author eleven books, including the 2003 smash hit *The Two Income Trap,* which she cowrote with her daughter.

Elizabeth Warren's famous persistence makes her one of the most well-known women in the race, and someone who ascended to become a vice chair of the Senate Democratic Caucus just four years into her political career.

Party activists tried to draft Warren to run for president during the 2016 primary because of her uniquely Midwestern flavor of firebrand populism fused with the progressive liberalism of her adopted hometown of Cambridge, Massachusetts, where she has resided since 1995. She instead campaigned for Hillary Clinton, later raising her national profile considerably after her stinging criticisms of the President during the 2016 election, which led to a running war of words with Donald Trump. Warren is projected to be one of the last Democrats standing, so it is sure to be a war that is just beginning.

Warren's politics are born of activism, and that activism led to the most significant economic reforms since the beginning of the twentieth century. Her advice was used to compose the Dodd-Frank Act, one of the most important financial reforms since the founding of the Securities and Exchange Commission in 1934. Congress likewise used her ideas to create the Consumer Financial Protection Bureau, one of the most significant consumer protection improvements in America since the 1914 founding of the Federal Trade Commission. This was all *before* she joined the US Senate.

However, Senator Warren's career as an activist started two decades earlier. In 1996, she switched her party allegiance from Republican to Democrat after Newt Gingrich's Contract for America flipped the House to GOP control for the first time in decades, and just as many Americans were moving to the right.

From 1995 through 2005, she vociferously opposed changes to the US bankruptcy system that would make it more difficult for families to get a fresh start, especially while the costs of health care and education skyrocketed for American families.

Unfortunately, Senate Republicans managed to push their bankruptcy "reform" act through Congress in the waning days of their total control of the federal government over Warren's vocal objections. In response, she redoubled her efforts to fight for debtor relief—efforts that elevated the plight of the American family to the top political issue of that decade. There is no question that if elected president, Senator Warren would use her place as a tough critic of banks and Wall Street to crack down on unjust lending practices.

Senator Warren's position on bankruptcy and the middle class and her other ideas on consumer protection became central elements of the 2008 Democratic presidential primary and that year's turbulent general election. By then her research, indicating that hundreds of thousands of families—even those with insurance—filed bankruptcy because of egregious medical bills, filtered out through the media and exerted a strong impact on the political landscape.

Then-candidate Obama criticized both his primary opponent, former Senator Hillary Clinton, and his GOP opponent, Senator John McCain, for their stance in favor of making it more difficult for families to file bankruptcy and discharge their debts.

"One of the basic principles in this economy and in this election is that when people are treated fairly and work is rewarded, and when there's some regulation of how financial systems operate, then economic growth happens from the bottom," Agence France-Presse reported[1] Barack Obama telling an audience during the Presidential campaign after he locked up the nomination, but before the Democratic National Convention, when he appeared at a panel in Chicago onstage with then-Professor Elizabeth Warren. "But when you have a system where only the top handful of CEOs on Wall Street are doing well and are allowed to take advantage of people, sooner or later our economy is going to break down."

President Obama's central campaign promise was to implement health insurance reform that ended policy cancellations and exceptions for "pre-existing conditions," made health care marketplaces for individuals, and expanded Medicare. It was a policy born of the very problems Senator Warren first identified.

But that was just prelude to Warren's biggest idea yet, one that would change the face of consumer finance across America. It has led to one of her greatest successes in office; helping millions of Wells Fargo customers escape the clutches of a national scam.

Warren's 2007 essay "Unsafe at Any Rate"[2] outlined her arguments in terms anyone could understand. Its subtitle says it all: "If it's good enough for microwaves, it's good enough for mortgages. Why we need a Financial Product Safety Commission."

Congress passed the Dodd-Frank Wall Street Reform and Consumer Protection Act in 2010, which included Warren's creation, named the Consumer Financial Protection Bureau. It is America's first one-stop shop to regulate every credit transaction that an average person encounters, from mortgages to credit cards to payday loans and even to bank accounts, and it has achieved results in just the few short years of its existence.

"Nobody fought harder for Wall Street reform; the reform that is now law and protecting consumers all across the country, than Elizabeth," President Obama told a Warren for Senate campaign rally in 2012, "reform that will end taxpayer bailouts, make sure folks aren't being taken advantage of by mortgage lenders and credit card companies."[3]

"She has been a fierce advocate since before I knew her for the middle class," Obama said. "She has been advocating on core issues that matter to families her entire career."

That won't change in 2020. Elevating the economic and consumer protection issues she's dedicated her career to studying is bound to be part of Senator Warren's plan to separate from the pack in the presidential primary.

Senator Warren's early campaign consists of progressive politics at its finest, including a proposed asset tax on the super wealthy, many of whom restructure their income so that they don't have to pay taxes. She has also introduced a new plan to break up the big tech companies as part of her plan to become America's foremost "trust buster" since President Teddy Roosevelt if she's elected to the job.

There is no question that Senator Warren's impact on the American financial landscape has been nothing short of monumental, but there are several questions on the impact that she will have on the 2020 Democratic presidential primary at its outset.

Her high-profile political opposition to President Trump has made her a hero with grassroots Democrats throughout the country, but some political missteps have given some pause about selecting her to be the top of the ticket in 2020.

Nobody could've imagined when she began her senatorial career that Elizabeth Warren's representations based upon family tales and oral history could take on a life of their own over the last two years, when she has come under fire with racist comments from President Trump. Her decision to pursue genetic testing into her Native American heritage and her subsequent release of that information diverted a substantial amount of political press attention from the senator, which could have otherwise been devoted to matters of her substantial proposals to improve the lives of ordinary American voters, which happens to be her real forte.

In addition, Senator Warren's attempts at using casual moments on social media have sometimes backfired. To be fair, even her social media-savvy opponents like former U.S. Rep. Beto O'Rourke have had their bad moments on social media, too.

In today's political climate, the question has become: Is it better to be known for the wrong reasons, simply because that means you're known?

Maybe.

Senator Warren also faces difficulty distinguishing herself as the top choice of the Democratic Party's progressive voters since Senator Bernie Sanders (I-VT) recently declared his candidacy and has taken full advantage of his large national fund-raising database. Warren raised $299,000 online within twenty-four hours of her campaign launch,[4] according to statistics from the Democratic fund-raising platform Act Blue, while Sanders brought in over twenty times that amount.

Unlike Senator Sanders, who has not much to speak of for major legislative accomplishments[5] and prefers his role to be that of ideologue, Warren can credibly claim multiple major policy wins before even starting in the Senate.

Not only that, but Senator Warren can genuinely claim to have a legitimate record of bipartisan legislative proposals and accomplishments— even during the first two years of the Trump administration. In just the last two years, she cosponsored and helped pass bills that combat the national opioid crisis, help federal workers save more of their paychecks, and aim to make it easier for America's veterans to obtain commercial driver's licenses.[6]

Senator Warren brings the most defined ideas to the table of any Democratic primary candidate seeking the 2020 presidential nomination and proven effectiveness in putting those ideas into practice. Warren drags some political baggage that gives rise to legitimate questions about her electability at the top of the ticket.

Nobody can say if Senator Warren will win the Democratic primary, but she promises to be a contender. And nobody will dispute that her story will be one of the most closely followed for the entire election cycle.

POLITICAL CAREER

U nlike the typical career politician, Elizabeth Warren's experiences as a law professor and author have propelled her from a typical upbringing in Oklahoma, where she was a registered Republican, to a congressional career as one of the foremost progressive Democrats in the Senate. Recently, she told *The Daily Beast*[1] that her work as a Harvard law professor specializing in bankruptcy research and consumer advocacy created much of the "intellectual foundation" for the Occupy movement, and she's right. The two defining moments in Warren's political career are unusual in that both of them happened before she won a political office.

First, it was Warren's book, *The Two-Income Trap,* that turned her from a top adviser in financial circles into a bestselling author whose observations about the rising struggles American families face began to permeate national politics. Second, she became the architect of a new, independent financial regulation agency that consolidated numerous far-flung federal financial watchdogs under a single roof.

The Two-Income Trap was a major turning point in her career, and it resulted in Warren transforming the narrative about the increasing struggles of middle-class families from a hodgepodge of disconnected anecdotes into a meaningful and fact-based economic analysis. Her work thoughtfully explained for the first time why rising bankruptcy filings reflected the difficulty American families bear to raise children and when our health care system failed them throughout the country.

Two years after the book was released, the professor emeritus at Harvard Law School appeared at the Senate Finance Committee to testify[2] against the last major federal bankruptcy bill to be signed into law, a bill which had bipartisan support in the Senate. Warren started her testimony by noting the numerous high-profile corporate bankruptcies that weren't being "reformed" versus the American families who would face more red tape, more rules, and less understanding if their family obligations cause them to drown in debt. She said:

> In the eight years since this bill was introduced, there has been a revolution in the data available to us. Unlike eight years ago, we need not have a theoretical debate about who uses the bankruptcy system.
>
> We now know that one million men and women are turning to bankruptcy each year in the aftermath of a serious medical problem, and three-quarters of them had health insurance at the onset of the illness that ultimately bankrupted them.
>
> We know that a family with children is nearly three times more likely to file for bankruptcy than their counterparts who have no children. And we know that now more children every year live through their parents' bankruptcy than live through their parents' divorce.

The bill passed anyway. The outcome of her testimony against the bill demonstrated the gap between facts and politics in America.

Nevertheless, she persisted.

Warren's next momentous act on the public stage came just two years later, in writing when she published an essay in *Democracy Journal*[3] called "Unsafe at Any Rate," which proposed a new, independent financial regulator for every financial company dealing directly with average people as borrowers. But it wasn't a straight path to its founding; instead she would take a watchdog role in the largest bank bailout in American history first.

Soon after publishing her plan, she was appointed to chair congressional oversight of bailout fund known as the TARP (Troubled Asset Relief Program). Warren exposed President Bush's final treasury secretary Hank Paulson forking over seventy-eight billion dollars more to banks—a direct state subsidy—by overvaluing the assets taxpayers bought to stabilize banks during the Great Recession by a whopping seventy-six billion dollars.[4] Her stellar performance overseeing the GOP-backed bailout led to her second keystone moment—building a new regulatory institution—which is her most lasting political legacy, to date.

Warren designed and built the Consumer Financial Protection Bureau as a special adviser to President Obama. Financial complexity has multiplied in modern times, ever since Wall Street's financial wizardry with high-interest-rate financial products like payday loans as well as mortgages and credit cards. America has never before had a single, centralized federal agency, just to protect people from predatory lending in all forms.

Since then, the senator become the leading legislator in holding America's too-big-to-fail banks accountable, and the agency she created has already caught and exposed major schemes.

A BOOK THAT DISCOVERED THE ROOT CAUSE OF MIDDLE-CLASS DISTRESS IN AMERICA

The number of bankruptcy filings in America began to steadily climb after the 1980s, but nobody else could figure out why.

Warren's book debunked the industry myth of the predatory consumer, replacing it with the reality that has defined her political career since then: the families who make up the American middle class are struggling to pay ever-increasing costs of living, driven by the necessity to pay top dollar to live near good schools and the crushing cost of health care. Not only that, but her book research even debunked her own suppositions about the financial health of families with multiple incomes.

"We thought that what we were going to find was that when families sent mothers back to work, those families would be more secure, and the data just didn't show that. So we thought, all right, maybe this is a story of overconsumption," Warren told CBS News' Hanna Storm in 2003[5] while discussing her book. "What the data actually showed is that families are spending far more on the basic expenses—the mortgage, health insurance, a second car so Mom can get to work, and tuition for nursery school and for college. It's these core expenses, the expenses that makes a family middle class, that's actually outside the reach of the average family."

"The problem here, the financial problem here is one that can be described as schools, schools, schools," said Warren. "Parents are desperate to try to stay in the public schools, but the only way they can do that is shop for public schools. And under the current laws, the only way you get to shop for a public school is by buying a house."

"The No. 1 increase for families from a generation ago to right now is what they're spending on mortgages. The cost of a mortgage for a median income family has gone up 70 times faster than a father's income, when adjusted for inflation on both sides." Warren told CNN's *American Morning* in a segment entitled 'Going Broke' with Bill Hemmer.[6] "What that really means is they've put Mom to work and put virtually all of her salary into trying to buy a decent house. And then behind that, there's health insurance, which has risen about 40 times faster than a father's income. There's the second car, so that mom can be at work. And there's the cost of daycare. . . . Rising fixed costs for middle income families ean that unless they learn how to play the game smarter, they will be part of the statistics that are the rising number of people in bankruptcy, the tripling of home mortgage foreclosures, the increase in the number of people who can't make this month's car payment or can't stay up with their credit card bills."

With just one book, Warren revolutionized how the American public perceived bankruptcy in an era when household debt skyrocketed. Indeed, it's not a stretch to say that her book kicked off the Democratic Party's continuing campaign to reform health insurance, which led to the Affordable Care Act (a.k.a. Obamacare) and eventually the call for single-payer health care in the 2020 primary.

"Today's families need to take a financial fire drill, even if they don't feel like they're in financial trouble," she told CNN's Hemmer while explaining a step-by-step approach to dealing with financial problems once they've ignited a family's financial picture. "We start out by telling families who are in serious financial trouble to know that you are not alone. . . . The second thing we tell a family in financial trouble is any family in trouble needs to think like a family at war. Think of the things you care about most, and protect those things. Pay those bills first. Don't pay attention to the noisiest creditor; pay attention to how to protect the assets you care most about. And the third thing we say is never try to borrow your way out of financial trouble. It won't work."

Unfortunately, millions of American families did not get Warren's warnings and did try to borrow their way out of debt just a couple of years later, aided by Wall Street's exotic financial schemes that led to an explosion of high-rate mortgage debt with few to no questions asked. That in turn led to a real estate bubble of high prices, when banks used only the value of the home to determine if a loan was worthy of being made or not.

Elizabeth Warren devoted an entire chapter of *The Two-Income Trap* to former Democratic presidential nominee Hillary Clinton's long and complicated relationship with America's bankruptcy laws, which shifted sharply once she got elected as the junior senator from New York. She met Clinton for the first time in 1998, and in a thirty-minute meeting, she convinced the first lady to kill a House Republican Congressman's bankruptcy bill which would've made it more difficult for families to seek relief from their creditors through the bankruptcy courts. The book recounted a three-page anecdote which reads like a prescient breakdown of the dividing lines in today's Democratic Party between its progressive and pro-business wings today, except that it was Hillary Clinton who exemplified both groups with her political decisions over the span of just a couple of years. Warren wrote:[7]

I have taught bankruptcy law to thousands of students—some of them among the brightest in the country—but I never saw one like Mrs. Clinton. Impatient, lightining-quick, an interested in all the nuances . . . At the end of our discussion, Mrs. Clinton stood up and said, "Well, I'm convinced. It is our job to stop that awful bill. You help me, and I'll help you."

Mrs. Clinton's newfound opposition to the bankruptcy bill surprised me. Given her legal training and her devotion to women's causes, I had certainly expected her to grasp the importance of the issue. But President Clinton's staff has been quietly supporting the bankruptcy bill for several months. Bill Clinton wanted to show that he and other "New Democrats" could play ball with business interests, and the major banks were lobbying hard for changes in the bankrutpcy laws. I had expected that it would take a lot more than thirty minutes to convince Hillary Clinton to depart from the position widely rumored to be supported by her husband.

But Mrs. Clinton stayed firm in her fight against "that awful bill." Over the ensuing months, she was true to her *word. With her strong support, the Democrats slowed the bill's passage through Congress. When Congress finally passed the bill in October 2000, President Clinton vetoed it.*

But the story doesn't end there. In the spring of 2001, the bankrutpcy bill was reintroduced in the Senate, essentially unchanged. . . . This time freshman Senator Hillary Clinton voted in favor of the bill. As First Lady, Mrs. Clinton had been persuaded that the bill was bad for families, and she was willing to fight for her beliefs. As New York's newest senator, however, it seems that Hillary Clinton could not afford such a principled decision.

"We now know that one million men and women are turning to bankruptcy each year in the aftermath of a serious medical problem, and three-quarters of them had health insurance at the onset of the illness that ultimately bankrupted them," Warren testified to the Senate in 2005, opposing the passage of that same "bankruptcy reforms" bill aimed at slamming the door on debt forgiveness for families and small businesses.

Warren told the Senate committee how major corporations had used Chapter 11 bankruptcy provisions to shirk pension plans and health-care coverage while paying tens of millions to "executives and insiders," while families with children became three times more likely to seek court protection from creditors than their childless counterparts. But the Bankruptcy Abuse Prevention and Consumer Protection Act of 2005 (BAPCPA) was explicitly designed to make it "more difficult for people to file for bankruptcy," according to its sponsor, Sen. Grassley, who openly lamented President Clinton's pocket veto due to Warren's previously successful efforts.[8]

While Warren's efforts slowed down the GOP-led efforts to pass the bill by a whopping six years, but Senator Chuck Grassley climatically forced the bill through the Senate in April 2005, just as his party's grip on Congress waned. The bill passed the House under Speaker Hastert's (R-IL) guidance, and President Bush signed it into law. Congress rebuked Elizabeth Warren's advocacy efforts by passing Grassley's bankruptcy bill in bipartisan fashion, but the GOP's greater failure to make America's economy a fair playing field only emboldened her political career.

Soon afterward, her political star began to rise in tandem alongside the fortunes of a then-junior senator from Illinois, a lawmaker who was one of only twenty-five legislators in his chamber to vote against the BAPCPA bill.

His name was Barack Obama.

THE IDEA BEHIND THE CONSUMER FINANCIAL PROTECTION BUREAU

Barely five years later, in a stunning reversal of fortune for Warren and an audacious rise to the presidency for him, President Obama appointed her to be his Special Advisor, the architect of the Consumer Financial Protection Bureau.

Warren's policy prescriptions became suddenly popular after the Bush era's radical deregulation crashed the American economy. The Democratic

Party surged back into power, winning all of the political branches of government, and they adopted her top idea for a single federal agency to defend consumers from unfair terms, and sometimes outright trickery, from financial companies.

It was long overdue.

America's financial system evolved over many decades with an alphabet soup of different regulators, each limited in scope and focused as more on the banks than the impact on their customers and borrowers.

"Unsafe at Any Rate" demonstrated Warren's unique combination of intellect, storytelling, and studious analysis. Her 5,388-word essay in some ways quite literally got turned into the Consumer Financial Protection Bureau. She began the story with this analogy to simplify a complex problem vexing millions of Americans:

> It is impossible to buy a toaster that has a one-in-five chance of bursting into flames and burning down your house. But it is possible to refinance an existing home with a mortgage that has the same one-in-five chance of putting the family out on the street—and the mortgage won't even carry a disclosure of that fact to the homeowner. Similarly, it's impossible to change the price on a toaster once it has been purchased. But long after the papers have been signed, it is possible to triple the price of the credit used to finance the purchase of that appliance, even if the customer meets all the credit terms, in full and on time.

Why are consumers safe when they purchase tangible consumer products with cash, but when they sign up for routine financial products like mortgages and credit cards they are left at the mercy of their creditors?

The difference between the two markets is regulation.

Financial regulation in America didn't even exist until the aftermath of the Great Depression moved Congress to act. As Warren noted in her essay, the Republican Party has turned the word "regulation" into a swear word, starting with President Reagan's election. For the ensuing four decades, the GOP has prominently included the principle of deregulation in their political platforms.

Warren probably knew that America was headed for a financial cliff as big and dangerous as the Great Depression when she wrote about the need for regulation in the summer of 2007. Within a few short years Democrats regained both houses of Congress, just as they did in the 1930s and likewise, they again chose to enact sensible regulations to save capitalism from itself.

Warren modeled her proposed "Financial Product Safety Commission" on the popular and uncontroversial U.S. Consumer Product Safety Commission (CPSC), which was founded by the Nixon administration in 1972. Her idea went beyond the boundaries of what Congress ultimately created, suggesting that the new agency even give preliminary review of mortgages and credit card plans before they're offered to consumers. While congressional Democrats didn't go that far, it's still important to note her reasoning behind strong consumer protections. She wrote:

An FPSC would promote the benefits of free markets by assuring that consumers can enter credit markets with confidence that the products they purchase meet minimum safety standards.

Companies that offer good products would have little to fear. Indeed, if they could conduct business without competing with companies whose business model involves misleading the customer, then the companies offering safer products would be more likely to flourish.

One of her key ideas about America's future consumer financial regulator should get involved in making uniform disclosures for all sorts of credit products, because regular citizens shouldn't have to become financial wizards just to get a credit card or take out a loan. She wrote:

A Commission might promote uniform disclosures that make it easier to compare products from one issuer to another, and to discern conflicts of interest on the part of a mortgage broker or seller of a currently loosely regulated financial product.

Amazingly, even the present management of the Consumer Financial Protection Bureau agrees with her assessment of the necessity of uniform disclosures to promote better outcomes for Americans who borrow money. CFPB Acting Deputy Director Brian Johnson, whom the *Wall Street Journal* noted is a former Republican congressional aide behind partisan attacks[9] on the agency, had this to say in late 2018[10] about the positive impact of uniform disclosures on market efficiency:

> [C]ompetition is necessary for a marketplace to function efficiently. Disclosure-based regulation reinforces market processes by ensuring consumers have access to truthful and understandable information.
>
> These types of disclosures allow consumers to more efficiently compare similarly-situated consumer products among different lenders and decide whether the product fits their needs. So the Bureau is helping to lead the charge toward efficient and effective disclosures that respect consumer autonomy and leverage the economy's high-tech advances. For instance, the Bureau's new Office of Innovation has proposed creating a BCFP Disclosure Sandbox to encourage companies to conduct trial disclosure programs.

Of course, Johnson proceeded in his speech to disagree strongly with Warren's toaster metaphor in that same speech. But it's notable how much common ground even a Trump administration appointee generally opposed to regulation found with the Harvard professor emeritus on one of the key cornerstones of consumer protection.

In the summer of 2010, the Dodd-Frank Wall Street Reform and Consumer Protection Act became law. It sought to remedy the conditions that led to the Bush era's "Great Recession," and turned Warren's FPSC into the Consumer Financial Protection Bureau, a tough cop on the beat to police financial abuses.

That's when President Obama hired Professor Warren away from her role as the head of congressional oversight for the bank bailout and placed her in charge of building the new consumer regulator on September 17, 2010 as a special adviser to the Treasury Department and Assistant to the President.[11] Obama told the press:[12]

> I am very grateful that Elizabeth has agreed to serve in this important role of getting the Consumer Financial Bureau up and running and making it as effective as possible.
>
> The Consumer Financial Protection Bureau will crack down on the abusive practices of unscrupulous mortgage lenders, reinforce the new credit card law we passed banning unfair rate hikes, and ensure that folks aren't unwittingly caught by overdraft fees when they sign up for a checking account. The Consumer Financial Protection Bureau will be a watchdog for the American consumer, charged with enforcing the toughest financial protections in history.

With that announcement, Warren embarked on the final stage of her journey from academia into national politics.

Less than a year later, Republican senators vehemently signaled that they would refuse to confirm her[13] to be the first head of the agency she designed, afraid of the kinds of financial frauds and abuses that she would find. They went so far as to gather forty-four signatures in a May 2011 letter opposing Warren's appointment to lead the CFPB unless she and President Obama agreed to significantly weaken the agency.

Little did GOP senators know that their obstinacy would propel Warren into their ranks. Just a month after the president made her non-nomination official, she launched an exploratory committee for her senatorial campaign. The first Draft Warren campaign (of what would become multiple efforts encouraging her to run) raised $100,000 to get her started in August 2011.[14]

"Unbeknownst to most of us, when Ted Kennedy died Harvard Law Professor Elizabeth Warren became the last liberal with balls," wrote[15] Elie Mystal, editor of the *Above the Law* news website about her campaign. "While other Democrats have been desperately trying to keep themselves in the good graces of Wall Street, Elizabeth Warren has been standing toe-to-toe with the bankers. It therefore seems only appropriate that Warren is now running for Ted Kennedy's old Senate Seat. . . ."

Elizabeth Warren's seventeen-year run as an outsider activist turned insider came to an end in November 2012 when she beat Republican Scott Brown, but those moments defined her political career in a manner that has carried over to her candidacy for president of the United States.

Senator Warren's presidential campaign platform already focuses on the kinds of kitchen-table issues she learned academically, and upon which she honed her talents as a writer and speaker.

More importantly, Senator Warren learned during her years as an activist both how to get things done in Washington and how to move the national political conversation during her extensive career as a crusading professor. Warren has already demonstrated the rare ability to move the needle on policy during her presidential campaign. It's a skill that is not easy to learn, but is utterly crucial to winning election to the Oval Office.

President Obama demonstrated a mastery of moving the political narrative with his speeches, but he based some of his most important campaign promises on Warren's ideas[16] about financial security for the middle class. While other candidates may speak in the abstract about the struggles of middle-class families, she literally wrote the book on why we need everything from the Affordable Care Act's guaranteed coverage to modern consumer protection and bank regulation.

Often, presidential candidates struggle to define themselves, and it's a problem that can be magnified in a crowded field of candidates such as the Democratic 2020 primary field. It's very rare for a junior senator to have major legislative accomplishments because the body tends to place significant value on seniority. That is also the main reason why none of Warren's opponents from the Senate have an accomplishment like founding the CFPB. Several of her opponents' primary experience has come as a mayor or governor, neither of which require the kind of national outlook that Warren mastered long ago.

Warren will have no problems defining her candidacy—neither ideologically, where she appeals to the liberal wing of her party, nor on the issues she has fought to change for the last twenty-four years. That's why the senator has already demonstrated her policy strength by doing something her competition won't do at this early stage of the race.

While some of her opponents are launching their campaigns without any publicly available policy ideas,[17] Warren's campaign is already taking the lead in making new, concrete policy proposals. These include a luxury tax on the wealthiest Americans and her plan to engineer more competition with less regulation in the tech sector by breaking up or restricting the largest tech companies.[18]

It's difficult to say if Elizabeth Warren's strategy will be politically advantageous, but in debates, she is definitely able to use an original policy platform against her opponents to distinguish her campaign.

CAMPAIGN PLATFORM

Senator Elizabeth Warren's academic background gives her campaign's policy platforms significant gravitas, which she distills into five main planks: ending corruption in Washington, rebuilding the middle class, strengthening our democracy, ensuring equal justice under the law, and building a "foreign policy for all."

In addition, Warren has introduced two major proposals that would change the way America's pervasive tech companies operate, and how we tax the wealthiest Americans.

Senator Warren's liberal ideology is apparent in the complete range of her policies from approval of sound regulation, her cosponsorship of a "Medicare for All" national health insurance proposal, and her plans to make our taxation system more progressive. No less an authority than *The Progressive* says that she's positioned herself as a "progressive champion"[1] early in the race.

When *Time* magazine asked Hillary Clinton to profile Warren for their 2015 list of America's 100 most influential people,[2] she wrote:

> *Elizabeth Warren never lets us forget that the work of taming Wall Street's irresponsible risk taking and reforming our financial system is far from finished. And she*

*never hesitates to hold powerful people's feet to the fire:
bankers, lobbyists, senior government officials and, yes,
even presidential aspirants.*

Political ideology aside, the senator's politics in Washington, DC, have been pragmatic. Her legislative record demonstrates an ability to work across the aisle to pass bipartisan legislation by consensus to achieve her goals, which often center on getting government to "save capitalism from itself."[3]

ENDING CORRUPTION IN WASHINGTON

Senator Warren's plan to expose the impact of special-interest lobbying and limit its reach is wholly contained in the ninety-eight-page bill she submitted during the 2017–2018 Congress entitled the Anti-Corruption and Public Integrity Act.[4]

"Our national crisis of faith in government boils down to this simple fact: People don't trust their government to do the right thing because they think government works for the rich, the powerful, and the well-connected, and not for the American people," she said at a press conference revealing the bill, according[5] to *Politico*. "And here's the kicker: They're right."

It's an ambitious plan to comprehensively limit the influence corporations purchase in the legislative and federal rulemaking process. It also seeks to establish a new Office of Public Integrity, create an oversight board for the Office of Congressional Ethics, levy an excise tax on the money paid to lobbyists which would fund the branches of government being lobbied, end foreign lobbying "as we know it," and other initiatives. The summary alone is six pages long, single-spaced,[6] but worth the read to anyone serious about reforming the influence of money in politics.

Her goals include locking the "revolving door" between government and lobbying, increasing public integrity, and ending lobbying as we know it. Many Americans would be shocked to learn that there is what amounts to a "shadow congress" consisting of 425 former legislators who stayed in Washington after leaving public service just to lobby the House and Senate,[7] such as former Senate leaders Bob Dole (R-KS) and Tom Daschle (D-SD). That's why one of the key features of Senator Warren's plan is to create a lifetime ban on lobbying by members of Congress, former Cabinet secretaries, federal judges, and even former vice presidents or presidents.

Senator Warren's plan would also turn corporate influence against itself in the federal rulemaking process, which is arcane to the average citizen. But federal rulemaking is very important, since executive departments like the US Department of Housing and Urban Development (HUD), and their agencies like the Federal Housing Administration (FHA), create lengthy rules to guide their activities where laws are silent. Her bill would direct a new excise tax on lobbying expenditures which would then be used to fund the same agencies who are being lobbied, in order to deal with the avalanche of special-interest lobbying dollars. It would additionally create a new Office of the Public Advocate just to assist the common citizen in giving more input to the federal rulemaking process.

Senator Warren's bill would contain major improvements to the federal judicial system's ethics requirements, and additionally a new code of conduct for the Supreme Court. It would even require federal courts to livestream audio of their proceedings, whereas most federal legal proceedings strictly ban video recording, and audio recordings are optional.[8]

The Anti-Corruption and Public Integrity Act would curb foreign lobbying by requiring the representatives of foreign corporations, governments, and political parties to register themselves solely under the Foreign Agents Registration Act. That's the same law President Trump's former campaign chairman was convicted of violating, and reporting requirements of Warren's proposed bill are much higher than what foreign lobbyists are currently required to use when working for overseas commercial interests.

Lobbyists would even have to disclose that they're registered—and for whom and why—under Warren's bill before they begin talking with public officials, which is a sea change from current practice. Her plan would also end the loopholes that allow members of Congress to engage in insider trading, extend ethics rules to all White House advisers, and strengthen the Freedom of Information Act to provide more public records to journalists and others who want to know what the government is doing.

If that wasn't enough, Warren's bill includes the Presidential Conflicts of Interest Act,[9] an initiative squarely aimed at preventing the conflicts of interest that President Trump carries by requiring all future presidents to place their holdings into a true blind trust and to release their tax returns.

"There is a danger that the spotlight on president Donald Trump's outrageous transgressions of ethics standards and unprecedented, global conflicts of interest will blind us to the more pervasive corporate corruption of our government," said Robert Weissman, president of the nonprofit watchdog group Public Citizen,[10] who endorsed Warren's bill. "No single reform, nor even any single set of reforms, can solve this problem. But Warren's bill would peel away layers of corruption."

Senator Warren attracted multiple House sponsors last year for her Anti-Corruption Act's companion bill,[11] including Rep. John Sarbanes (D-MD). He is the author and primary sponsor of the 2019–2020 Congress's H.R. 1 government reform bill, which expands voting rights and works to expose dark money in politics.

Elizabeth Warren's plan to reform the ways of Washington to return power to the people demonstrates her detailed knowledge of the legislative process from the inside and outside, as well as a grasp of the numerous ways that corporations buy influence from federal employees and former elected officials.

REBUILDING THE MIDDLE CLASS

Elizabeth Warren's plan to restore America's middle class rests upon making federal taxes more progressive to pay for a universal child care program, providing student debt relief, and creating 1.5 million jobs while simultaneously lowering the cost of rent across the country.

It all starts with her tax plan to institute an "Ultra-Millionaire tax"[12] aimed at raising significant revenue from the 75,000 wealthiest families in America in order to restore the progressive tax system which the IRS says that America's income tax is based upon.[13] However, the American tax code has been inverted to a regressive plan that benefits the ultra wealthy, largely due to decades of lobbying and the sway of big dollar political donations.

The IRS defines a progressive taxation system as taking "a larger percentage of income from high-income groups than from low-income groups and is based on the concept of ability to pay." But research from a pair University of California, Berkeley economists published on Warren's campaign website,[14] demonstrates that families in the top 0.1 percent of earners only pay 3.2 percent of their net worths toward income taxes on average. Most American families, 99 percent of lower-income households to be exact, pay 7.2 percent of their household net worths in income taxes annually.

Warren's proposal would only raise the amount that America's wealthiest taxpayers owe by 1 percent of their net worths annually, but her campaign says that it would be enough to pay for universal child care,[15] or any number of proposals including student loan debt relief. She also terms her tax plan "a down payment on" the "idea" of Green New Deal[16] to combat climate change as proposed by Rep. Alexandria Ocasio-Cortez (D-NY). Her campaign website distills the Warren tax plan down to just four bullet points:

- Zero additional tax on any household with a net worth of less than $50 million (99.9% of American households)
- Two percent annual tax on household net worth between $50 million and $1 billion
- One percent annual Billionaire Surtax (3% tax overall) on household net worth above $1 billion

- Ten-year revenue total of $2.75 trillion (estimate by UC Berkeley professors)

"Consider two people: an heir with $500 million in yachts, jewelry, and fine art, and a teacher with no savings in the bank," Warren notes on her website in an illustration of the unequal tax burden of our current income-tax system in the real world. "If both the heir and the teacher bring home $50,000 in labor income next year, they would pay the same amount in federal taxes, despite their vastly different circumstances. Increasing income taxes won't address this problem."

Once the federal government adds new revenues under the Warren tax plan, it would then be able to help struggling families across America under the senator's universal child care and early learning plan.[17]

Young families sorely need the help.

U.S. News and World Report ranks the United States as the twentieth-best country in which to raise a family,[18] just ahead of Greece and Poland, even though our country's per capita income is higher than all but four of the higher-ranked nations.

"When people say, 'That's going to be really expensive'—yes, it is: This will be about four times more than we have invested in our children, but that's exactly what we need to do," Ms. Warren said at a rally on March 18, 2019, according[19] to the *New York Times*. "I am so tired of hearing what the richest country on the face of the earth just can't afford to do."

Warren's plan to assist parents will use a progressive means test to make child care free for parents who earn less than 200 percent of the federal poverty level,[20] which would start at $24,980 for a single-child household up to $86,860 for a family with eight kids. Everyone else would pay no more than 7 percent of their income to get comprehensive child care, and this is how her campaign website says it would work:

- The federal government will partner with local providers—states, cities, school districts, nonprofits, tribes, faith-based organizations—to create a network of child care options that would be available to every family.
- These options would include locally licensed child care centers, preschool centers, and in-home child care options.
- Local communities would be in charge, but providers would be held to high national standards to make sure that no matter where you live, your child will have access to quality care and early learning.
- Child care and preschool workers will be doing the educational work that teachers do, so they will be paid like comparable public school teachers.

The plan is based upon the successful Head Start program,[21] which President Lyndon B. Johnson enacted in the 1960s as part of his "Great Society" program, and the US military's current universal child care program. Moody's Analytics Chief Economist Mark Zandi and Managing Director Sophia Koropeckyj published an independent analysis[22] of Warren's plan, which estimates that 5.2 million additional American children will receive child care if it's enacted, while only 6.8 million children are currently in comparable programs today. Moody's economic analysis concluded that Warren's plan is "fiscally responsible" and would create a significant number of jobs. They wrote:

> The proposal quickly lifts economic growth, as the stimulus created by providing financial support to lower-income and middle-class families more than offsets the negative fallout from increasing taxes on the very wealthy.

> The proposal significantly reduces the cost burden of child care for most families, improves the quality of child care, enhances childhood development, and supports increased labor force participation and stronger economic growth.

> It is fiscally responsible proposal that would scale up federal child care programs that are already in place and shown to be effective in meeting the challenges of providing high-quality child care.

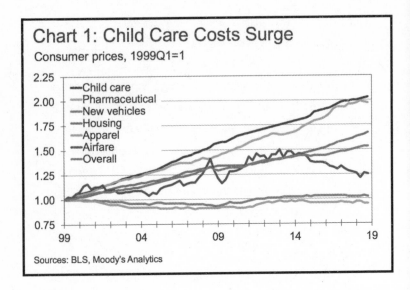

Chart 1: Child Care Costs Surge

Consumer prices, 1999Q1=1

- Child care
- Pharmaceutical
- New vehicles
- Housing
- Apparel
- Airfare
- Overall

Sources: BLS, Moody's Analytics

"No one builds a future without investment," said Senator Warren in October 2018,[23] and she told a CNN Town Hall with Jake Tapper[24] early in 2019 that her Ultra-Wealth Tax would take in four times the cost of her universal child care plan. "Whether you and I have small children or not, we have an interest in the future of this country, and that means we have an interest, and a responsibility to invest in America's children."

Senator Warren has also proposed a plan[25] to increase our national housing stock significantly which is aimed at giving every American a safe and affordable place to live. Her plan would lower rents nationwide 10 percent over the next decade, according to an independent analysis by Moody's Mark Zandi,[26] and create 1,500,000 new jobs. Zandi wrote:

Under the new legislation, our model shows that affordable housing construction increases by close to 200,000 units in 2019, to almost 250,000 units in 2020, and to 300,000 units in 2021.[27] Over the 10-year budget horizon through 2028, affordable housing production increases by about 300,000 units per annum. This is approximately equal to the current annual shortfall in housing supply.

Low- and middle-income households are struggling to make their rent and mortgage payments, suffering through increasingly long commutes, and unable to take better jobs because they cannot afford housing near the available work. The American Housing and Economic Mobility Act will go a long way toward addressing these problems. It is fiscally responsible legislation that empowers programs that are already in place and shown to be effective in meeting the challenges of providing affordable housing to low- and middle-income households and underserved communities.

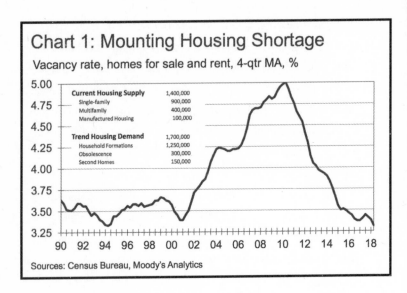

Chart 1: Mounting Housing Shortage

Vacancy rate, homes for sale and rent, 4-qtr MA, %

Current Housing Supply	
Single-family	900,000
Multifamily	400,000
Manufactured Housing	100,000
Total	1,400,000

Trend Housing Demand	
Household Formations	1,250,000
Obsolescence	300,000
Second Homes	150,000
Total	1,700,000

Sources: Census Bureau, Moody's Analytics

The centerpiece of Warren's efforts would be to spend the bulk of new funding on a pair of existing housing trust funds established by the Housing and Economic Recovery Act (HERA) of 2008, which right now only receive a few hundred million dollars a year from fees generated by national mortgage agencies Fannie Mae and Freddie Mac.[28]

Her plan would invest fifty billion dollars annually into developing affordable housing, with an emphasis on rural housing, giving assistance to homeowners who are still underwater in their homes from the Great Recession. It would also fund a new Middle-Class Housing Emergency Fund and attempt to fund 200,000 homes on tribal lands for Native Americans and Native Hawaiians.

"How would we pay for this new investment?" Warren asks on her website. "Currently, an heir doesn't pay a dollar of estate taxes until they inherit a fortune of $22 million or more. I would lower that threshold to $7 million—which is where it was when President George W. Bush left office—and raise the tax rates above that threshold so ultra-millionaires and billionaires pay a larger share. Those changes affect only 14,000 of the wealthiest families each year, but according to the Moody's analysis, they fully cover the cost of my plan." Not only that, but Zandi's expert analysis concluded that increasing estate taxes will have "little impact on the economy and jobs" because "wealthy households that will pay more in estate taxes have substantial financial resources and will not significantly change their spending and saving behavior."

If that wasn't enough, her plan seeks to create what *Slate* calls[29] the first new proposal to rectify racial disparities in housing since the Civil Rights era's Fair Housing Act—which President Trump was sued for violating by the Department of Justice—by providing down-payment assistance to families who live in areas that were targeted by the discriminatory practice known as "redlining."[30] Three-quarters of redlined neighborhoods remain low-income and nearly two-thirds of those neighborhoods still have majority minority populations, where Warren plans to make available down-payment grants for moderate- to low-income first-time homebuyers to obtain FHA loans.

In addition, Warren wants to extend the Fair Housing Act's anti-discrimination provisions to prohibit "housing discrimination on the basis of sexual orientation, gender identity, marital status, veteran status, and the source of one's income, like a housing voucher."

Finally, Senator Warren wants to strengthen antitrust enforcement substantially and has put forth a plan to break up America's largest technology companies[31] or restrict their business practices to level the playing field for small businesses.

"Firstly, by passing legislation that requires large tech platforms to be designated as 'Platform Utilities' and broken apart from any participant on that platform. Second," Warren says she "would appoint regulators committed to reversing illegal and anti-competitive tech mergers."

As examples of the mergers and acquisitions she'd like to unwind, her campaign website lists Facebook's purchase of the WhatsApp messenger and the Instagram social network, as well as Amazon's purchase of Zappos and Whole Foods.

The Warren for President Campaign tried to advertise that very plan on Facebook on March 11, 2019 with a post that read:

> *Three companies have vast power over our economy and our democracy. Facebook, Amazon, and Google. We all use them. But in their rise to power, they've bulldozed competition, used our private information for profit, and tilted the playing field in their favor. It's time to break up these big companies so they don't have so much power over everyone else. If you agree, add your name now.*

Facebook took down the ad, which linked to a petition seeking to break up the big tech companies.[32] Senator Warren believed that the national headlines over the spat made her point entirely about the need to increase regulation of the way large social networks conduct business. She tweeted:[33]

> *Curious why I think FB has too much power? Let's start with their ability to shut down a debate over whether FB has too much power. Thanks for restoring my posts. But I want a social media marketplace that isn't dominated by a single censor.*

Her website is careful to note that none of the tech companies she wants to regulate would go away, just that they would have to stop using their platforms to lock out small businesses, in addition to giving people more control over how their personal information is collected, shared, and sold.

STRENGTHENING OUR DEMOCRACY

Senator Warren's campaign promises to strengthen America's democracy with a mixture of reforms including getting rid of the electoral college, supporting House Democrats who just passed a major reform to end partisan gerrymandering in the For the People Act of 2019[34] (best known as HR1), and her twin goals of ending foreign election interference and eliminating racial disparities that keep minorities from voting.

"Politicians are supposed to compete over how many voters they can persuade, not how many citizens they can disqualify or demoralize," Warren's campaign website explains. "We must eliminate unnecessary and unjustified rules that make voting more difficult, and overturn every single voter suppression rule that racist politicians use to steal votes from people of color."

In addition, Warren supports a constitutional amendment to overturn the *Citizens United* decision, the Supreme Court case which more than tripled the amount of money flowing through outside expenditure groups to over a trillion dollars[35] from 2010 to 2018.

Her highest-profile statements about fixing America's election systems came at a recent CNN town hall with Jake Tapper in Jackson, Mississippi, a place which gets relatively little attention from presidential nominees because of its solidly Republican political makeup.

"We need to make sure that every vote counts. And, you know, I want to . . . push that right here in Mississippi, because I think this is an important point. You know, come a general election, presidential candidates don't come to places like Mississippi. They also don't come to places like California and Massachusetts, right? Because we're not the 'battleground states,'" she told the audience at Jackson State University, who responded to her last sentence with uproarious applause. "Well, my view is that every vote matters. And the way we can make that happen is that we can have national voting. And that means get rid of the Electoral College and everybody counts."

"I get that we have a lot of differences," Warren later told a questioner who identified himself as a Bernie Sanders supporter. "There will be some people who have a little more money, some people who have a little less, some people who go further in school, some people who don't. But the one thing we should all own an equal share of is an equal share of our democracy."

A FOREIGN POLICY FOR ALL

The final major plank of Elizabeth Warren's campaign platform is foreign policy, which focuses on rebuilding our alliances, "ending endless wars," and changing the terms of America's international trade to expand benefits for the middle class.

The Trump administration has hollowed out America's State Department,[36] slashing jobs and convincing experienced diplomats to retire, a trend that Senator Warren pledges to reverse. She wrote about how that would work[37] in the *Foreign Affairs* magazine published by the prestigious nonprofit and nonpartisan Council on Foreign Relations:

> *It will be essential to reprioritize diplomacy and reinvest in the State Department and the development agencies; foreign policy should not be run out of the Pentagon alone. The United States spends only about one percent of its federal budget on foreign aid. Some Americans struggling to make ends meet understandably question the value of U.S. commitments and contributions abroad, and certainly we should expect our partners to pay their fair share.*
>
> *But diplomacy is not about charity; it is about advancing U.S. interests and preventing problems from morphing into costly wars. Similarly, alliances are not exclusively about principles; they are about safety in numbers. The world is a big, complicated place, and not even the*

strongest nation can solve everything on its own. As we face down antidemocratic forces around the world, we will need our allies on our side.

Warren's plan to rebuild the State Department is in the mainstream of establishment policy ideas. So is the central thesis of her foreign policy, which is to rebuild America's national unity and invest in its people, which she explained in *Foreign Affairs*:

President John F. Kennedy, whose seat in the U.S. Senate I now hold, once wrote that "a nation can be no stronger abroad than she is at home." With American power increasingly challenged from within and without, we can no longer afford to think of our domestic agenda as separate from our foreign policy. A stronger economy, a healthier democracy, and a united people—these are the engines that power the nation and will project American strength and values throughout the world.

Every day, shortsighted domestic policies weaken American national strength. The United States is in the midst of a reverse-Sputnik moment, reducing investments in education and scientific research even as potential adversaries expand them.

Warren wants to "end endless war" which she accurately laments have been charged "to a collective credit card for future generations to pay" that happened when President George W. Bush became the first president to take America to war and cut taxes[38] (excluding the special case of Vietnam), while embarking on his "war of choice" to invade Iraq. In fact, the first income taxes in American history were raised to pay for war expenses.[39]

Warren wrote in *Foreign Affairs* about what she's learned from having three brothers who served in the military and what she's learned while sitting on the Senate Armed Services Committee:

> *A foreign policy that works for all Americans must also be driven by honest assessments of the full costs and risks associated with going to war. It is the job of the U.S. government to do what is necessary to protect Americans, but it is long past time to start asking what truly makes the country safer—and what does not. Military efforts alone will never fully succeed at ending terrorism, because it is not possible to fight one's way out of extremism.*
>
> *As a member of the Senate Armed Services Committee, I have seen up close how 17 years of conflict have degraded equipment, sapped forces' readiness, and forced the postponement of investment in critical military capabilities. It has distracted Washington from growing dangers in other parts of the world: a long-term struggle for power in Asia, a revanchist Russia that threatens Europe, and looming unrest in the Western Hemisphere, including a collapsing state in Venezuela that threatens to disrupt its neighbors. Would-be rivals, for their part,*

have watched and learned, and they are hard at work developing technologies and tactics to leapfrog the United States.

Ultimately, Bush's war in Iraq destabilized the Middle East, leading to the rise of the terrorist group ISIS and the current multistate war in Syria, both of which Warren believes that we can't solve with military force alone.

Senator Warren opposes President Trump's "NAFTA 2.0" agreement and wants to "produce a better deal for America's working families." In August 2018, she explained one of the biggest downsides of the current North American Free Trade Agreement (NAFTA) to CNBC's Jim Cramer:[40]

I am worried about trade policy that has been written largely by a handful of multinational corporations. I'll give you one quick example, and that's enforcement of promises in the trade deals. You know they put labor promises in, they put environmental promises in, they put the level-playing field promises in those trade deals; good luck getting them enforced.

But, for the giant multi-nationals there's a special, special deal. And the special deal is, if they don't like a new regulation that gets passed after they've cut a trade deal. They get to go to a special fast-track arbitration outfit made up of corporate lawyers. They come in and make their case that Canada shouldn't be able to prohibit this particular chemical or the United States is doing "X" or Mexico is doing "Y"; that they don't like that it cuts into corporate profits. A handful of corporate lawyers make a decision—and are you ready?—they hand down that decision, and either the country changes its law or makes a big payment. No going through a court system, no appeals, no nothing.

That's saying in effect: trade deals are written for the guys that run these big multinationals, not for the American people.

In addition to the corporate-friendly bent of NAFTA's international dispute process, Warren cites two key problems plaguing the global economy: employee dislocation and the illicit movement of ill-gotten cash and corruption. She wrote in *Foreign Policy*:

Job training and transition assistance proved powerless against the onslaught of offshoring, providing little more than burial insurance for workers who lost their jobs.

And as capital became more mobile, corporations and wealthy individuals sent trillions of dollars to offshore tax havens, robbing the U.S. government of needed resources to reinvest at home.

"We need to have more financial transparency." says James S. Henry, Esq. an investigative economist with the Tax Justice Network and a Global Justice Fellow at Yale who is a leading expert on money laundering. "If you're going to have a wealth tax, then you have to worry about people moving money secretly across different offshore tax havens. It will require policy goals like beneficial ownership registration, automatic information exchange among tax authorities—which the United States has so far refused to do—and you need country by country recording for corporate profits."

"Secondly, you have to work with other countries to accomplish those goals," says Henry, who is a contributing editor for the *American Interest*. "The territorial income tax in the Trump tax bill (which Republicans passed at the end of 2017) allows foreign operating subsidiaries of U.S. companies, which are more than 10 percent owned by American corporations, to not be required to file taxes on offshore income, which is decimating U.S. tax collection and ballooning the national deficit without generating economic growth."[41]

While Warren freely admits[42] that "the globalization of trade has opened up opportunity and lifted billions out of poverty around the world," which contrasts with the furthest left-wing elements of the Democratic Party, she decries the distribution of that wealth to corporations at the expense of workers.

Interestingly, the senator's policy on tariffs is closer to that of President Trump than those of most Democratic *and* Republican politicians. On March 11, 2017, she told CNN's Jim Acosta:

> What I'd like to see us do is rethink all of our trade policy. And I have to say, when President Trump says he's putting tariffs on the table, I think tariffs are one part of reworking our trade policy overall. We need a trade

> *policy that's comprehensive, one that makes a distinction between the trading partners that follow the rules and the trading partners that break the rules like China, but a comprehensive trade strategy that isn't all about multinational corporations' profits, that's really about American workers and American small businesses.*

Lastly, her policy on Russia would provide a sharp contrasting point with President Trump if they were to face off in a general election in 2020. Warren voted for sanctions and recently pressed the president in public to take a tougher stance toward Russia's recent provocations with its neighbor Ukraine.[43]

OTHER POLICIES

Elizabeth Warren is in favor of fighting climate change and has a 99 percent lifetime score in the Senate[44] from the League of Conservation Voters,[45] who rated ninety-two of her votes over a six-year period as pro-environment.

She introduced the Climate Risk Disclosure Act on September 17, 2018, and it was cosponsored[46] by seven Democratic senators, including her opponents Senator Cory Booker (D-NJ), Senator Kamala Harris (D-CA), and Senator Kirsten Gillibrand (D-NY). It's not a scientific climate-change bill, but it is the kind of pragmatic business legislation that Senator Warren has managed to pass in a bipartisan manner over the last six years, which smartly lays the groundwork for bigger policy adjustments later on.

"Our bill will use market forces to speed up the transition from fossil fuels to cleaner energy—reducing the odds of an environmental and financial disaster without spending a dime of taxpayer money," she said about the bill, which is a progressive idea to help investors price climate change into the stock market. But it's a free-market solution from the senator that comes wrapped in the kind of attractive political packaging you'll find in the Republican Party's platform[47] about free markets and even from House Republican representatives from across the country.[48]

Elizabeth Warren's smart outlook about the use of legislation to affect markets by requiring the largest public companies to measure and disclose the kind of statistics needed to build a case for changing climate-change policy. It would even give public companies a free-market incentive, in this case higher valuations, to advocate new climate-change policies. This bill demonstrates how the senator would approach the presidency with a fact-based bipartisan solution to a big problem impacting businesses across the country, and in a way that helps shareholders and doesn't require the federal government to do all of the work.

Another business reform bill Warren is proposing would create a requirement for 40 percent of the board seats of all large U.S. corporations to be held by workers. The Accountable Capitalism Act,[49] which Senator Warren introduced in August 2018, borrows from best practices around the globe to create a new federal charter for America's largest corporations. Her bill incorporates a concept which the founder of the financial advisory giant Vanguard Group wrote in a *New York Times* opinion editorial:[50] requiring companies to execute a vote for 75 percent of their boards in order to authorize political expenditures. Finally, it would give state attorneys general the power[51] to submit an administrative petition seeking the orderly corporate dissolution of any U.S. corporation—as they would be called—which is repeatedly punished for illegal behavior and gross disregard of the law. A U.S. corporation could appeal their punishment to Congress, thereby giving power back to the people to closely regulate some of America's worst corporate citizens.

In mid-2018, Senator Warren and Senator Cory Gardner (R-CO) cosponsored a bipartisan bill called the STATES Act,[52] which would've formally ended federal marijuana prosecutions in states that have legalized recreational or medicinal use. The bill would've also created a twenty-one-year-old national minimum age for buying recreational weed and legalized banking for marijuana businesses. Both senators hail from states that have legalized recreational weed, and the Republican senator from Colorado even told Bloomberg News[53] that they had the votes to pass the bill in late 2018, but it never got brought up for a vote.

Every single challenger for president in 2020—in both parties—supports some form of marijuana legalization, according[54] to the *Boston Globe*. Even President Trump is on the record in favor of letting states decide—though he has hired significant anti-marijuana crusaders like former Attorney General Jeff Sessions—which tracks with the goals of Warren's bill.

Senator Warren's stances on other issues regularly hew to Democratic Party lines. She is in favor of commonsense gun reforms, with which the entire 2020 Democratic primary field agrees.[55] She supports fixing the holes that President Trump and the last Republican-controlled Congress punched in health care coverage under the Affordable Care Act.

Senator Warren and her 2020 primary opponent Senator Harris recently cosponsored a Medicare for All bill which would create a single-payer public health insurance option, but would not outlaw private competition as Senator Sanders wishes to do.[56] Centrist Democratic candidates like Minnesota senator Amy Klobuchar, Governor Jay Inslee (WA), Governor John Hickenlooper (CO), and former Rep. John Delaney (MD) aren't in favor of Medicare for All as the public option. The centrists aren't in favor of national health insurance as advocated by Sanders, but all of them include some form of universal health care in their platforms.[57]

Warren is in favor of opening up a national conversation about slavery reparations, which is in line with the left wing of the Democratic Party's policies of fighting discrimination in its many forms. The senator opposes the Trump administration's policy of family separation that leaves kids in cages and parents of refugees guessing where their children have landed. Additionally, she has backed the movement to break up U.S. Immigration and Customs Enforcement (ICE) and replace[58] it with "something that reflects our morality." Progressive Democrats have raised call to "Abolish ICE" in the last year to express that they wish to restructure the agency to separate its law enforcement investigations division from the enforcement and deportation division.

She also fiercely opposed the nomination of Judge Brett Kavanaugh to the Supreme Court and even attended a protest against him,[59] rousing the crowd at a large rally in Washington by saying, "I watched that hearing last Thursday and I believe Dr. Ford. This is about power. I watched eleven men, powerful men, who tried to help another powerful man make it to an even more powerful position. This is about hijacking democracy. Let's be clear about this, I am angry and I own it. I am angry on behalf of women who have been told to sit down and shut up one time too many."

 **ABC News Politics** ✔
@ABCPolitics

Following ⌄

"I am angry on behalf of women who have been told to sit down and shut up."

Sen. Elizabeth Warren joins anti-Kavanaugh protesters in Washington, D.C.: "I believe Dr. Ford. I watched that hearing last Thursday and Brett Kavanaugh is disqualified" abcn.ws/2O1B5xQ

Video
See the whole picture with @ABC News.

12:42 PM - 4 Oct 2018

95 Retweets **183** Likes

💬 34 🔁 95 ⬢ ♡ 183 ✉

Elizabeth Warren's policies put her squarely in the Democratic field's left wing, which is a territory that is dominated in the polls early by Vermont Senator Bernie Sanders and sought by Senators Kamala Harris and Gillibrand, as well as up-and-coming South Bend, Indiana, Mayor Pete Buttigeig. Warren is well to the left of former vice president Joe Biden and Senator Amy Klobuchar, who are aiming squarely for the party's moderate wing of voters.

The senator will draw her greatest contrast with progressive opponents like Sanders and Rep. Tulsi Gabbard (D-HI) by pointing out her bipartisan accomplishments. It's likely that Warren will stress their sometimes substantial differences in foreign policy, where she is more or less aligned with mainstream Democratic thought. For example, Sanders supported Venezuela's socialist regime for many years until its recent collapse, and Gabbard has visited Syria's dictator Bashar al-Assad and still supports or refuses to condemn his brutal regime for committing war crimes.

Warren will likely stress the boldness of her domestic policy plans to correct income inequality when debating her adversaries in the moderate and centrist wing of the Democratic primary, such as Biden or Senator Cory Booker (NJ), who has taken significant donations from large pharmaceutical companies and defended the private equity industry from Democratic attacks while mayor of Newark.

Senator Warren has presented the most comprehensive set of domestic policies and plans of any of the candidates in early 2019. That makes it her top political challenge to distill those vast works into a platform that is easy for the average person to digest and attracts the average Democratic primary voter. She will need to find a way to make her platform appetizing to moderate and centrist independent voters, because that's the only way she will be able to defeat the eventual Republican candidate in the November 3, 2020, general election.

BIOGRAPHY: FORMATIVE BACKGROUND AND EDUCATION

Senator Warren's long journey to Washington, DC, began in Oklahoma before going to Harvard by way of the University of Houston, Rutgers University Law School, the University of Texas, University of Michigan, and the University of Pennsylvania. She was born Elizabeth Ann Herring on June 22, 1949, in Oklahoma City, Oklahoma, as the fourth and final child in her family. Warren's three older brothers John, Don Jr., and David Herring[1] are all military veterans.

She grew up in nearby Norman, Oklahoma, as part of a working-class family who eventually moved to Oklahoma City so Warren could attend better middle schools and high schools when she was eleven years old. Her father Don Sr. worked as a rug salesman at the Montgomery Ward department store until she was twelve, when disaster struck.

The Herring family's struggles have become one of Elizabeth Warren's cornerstone memories, an event which introduced her to the world of household finance, in which she has since become a leading expert. She recounted the story to CNN at a 2020 presidential town hall event:

And about the time I was in middle school, my daddy had a heart attack, and it was serious. Thought he was going to die. The church neighbors brought covered dishes. It was a scary time. He survived, but he couldn't go back to work. And we lost our family's station wagon. And at night, I'd hear my parents talk, and that's where I learned words like "mortgage" and "foreclosure."

And I remember the day that I walked into my parents' bedroom and laying out on the bed is the dress. And some people here will know the dress. It's the one that only comes out for weddings, funerals, and graduations. And my mother is in her slip, and she's stocking feet, and she's pacing back and forth, and she's crying. She's saying, "We will not lose this house. We will not lose this house." She was 50 years old. She had never worked outside the home. She was truly terrified.

And I watched her while she finally just pulled it together, put that dress on, put on her high heels, blew her nose, and walked to the Sears and got a minimum wage job. And that minimum wage job saved our house, but more importantly, it saved our family.

Her family lost their car, and Warren went to work waiting tables at her aunt's restaurant.

Unexpectedly, one small part of Warren's family lore has grown to politically overshadow the story of her typically American upbringing. In the 1940s, long before the internet placed genealogy databases into ubiquitous cellphones, the Herring family opposed her father Don's marriage to her mother Polly on the grounds that she was of Native American heritage, according[2] to her family's oral history:

> Back then, that was a big dividing line. For over a century, a major goal of federal policy was to assimilate Native people into society, without appreciation for their culture, traditions, or practices. Discrimination against Native people was common at the time. In 1932, when Elizabeth's mother was 19 and her father was 20, they eloped.

She listed herself as Native American several times throughout her academic career, though neither Warren nor her family ever enrolled in a tribe which determines citizenship. Eventually, it became a campaign issue in her first run for Senate in 2012.

At age sixteen, Warren earned a debate scholarship to George Washington University, where she enrolled at age seventeen. But in 1968, she left school at age nineteen to marry her high school sweetheart, mathematician Jim Warren, who worked for IBM at Houston's Johnson Space Center.[3] Her studies continued at the University of Houston—a commuter school—and she was awarded a degree in speech pathology in 1970.

Elizabeth Warren's plan was to be a special education teacher. She took a job in the field under a "temporary teaching certificate" for a year and then enrolled in graduate school[4] to obtain credits to finalize her certificate, before giving up on teaching. Her husband's job took her to New

Jersey, where she became pregnant with Amelia, who later coauthored *The Two-Income Trap*.

When her daughter turned two, Warren enrolled in Rutgers University Law School while juggling a traditional wife's role in the home. The year before she graduated, Warren interned for three months at 2 Wall Street for one of its oldest law firms, Cadwalader, Wickersham & Taft.[5] But she was pregnant with her second child, Alex, who was born soon after she graduated law school and couldn't land a job. She began practicing civil law when her alma mater called her and asked her to be a substitute professor in their law school.

Elizabeth Warren's marriage to Jim didn't work out, and they got divorced in 1978. She moved back to Houston to be a professor at the University of Houston Law School, where she rose to become Associate Dean for Academic Affairs in 1981. But it wasn't easy, and she recounts the story frequently when discussing her plan for universal child care; after six months as a law professor she nearly quit because of the struggle to find help with her daughter Amelia. In the end, her Aunt Bee stepped into the void and lived with Warren for fifteen years.

Elizabeth Warren met her second husband, Bruce Mann, at the University of Houston, but kept her first married name. He is also a law professor as well as a legal historian, and he has been the Carl F. Schipper, Jr. Professor of Law at Harvard since 2006.

After Warren had earned tenure at UH, she got a new job in 1983 at the prestigious University of Texas at Austin, where she would remain through 1987. Warren was raised in the Methodist Church, and even taught Sunday School during those four years.[6] That's where she began the speciality in bankruptcy that would propel her journey to the Ivy League and eventually the Senate.

Warren started teaching at the University of Pennsylvania in 1987, along with her husband Bruce. Her academic writing continued to grow her reputation until Harvard Law School offered her a one-year visiting professorship in 1992. Three years later, Harvard hired her to be the Leo Gottlieb Professor of Law, a position she held until her election to the Senate in 2012. She still holds the title of professor emeritus at Harvard Law.[7]

She is still married to Bruce Mann, and she has three grandchildren[8] and a golden retriever named Bailey.[9]

 **Elizabeth Warren** @ewarren

Following

My grandkids make me feel like the luckiest Gammy in the world. I was tickled to have them with me in Los Angeles last weekend!

WWW.ELIZABETHWARREN.COM

WARREN

TEXT FIGHT TO 24477

And that's why I want her

5:43 PM - 2 Mar 2019

1,539 Retweets 10,375 Likes

434   1.5K   10K

CREDENTIALS: PUBLIC SERVICE AND POLITICAL CAREER

Elizabeth Warren's academic résumé[1] detailing her extensive writing and public service from the mid 1970s through her 2012 senatorial race is lengthy, and it outlines her journey from writing for the *Rutgers Law Review* review while she was a second-year law student all the way through her op-eds in the *New York Times*.

Warren's focus in academia was teaching law students about the nuts and bolts of America's capitalist system with a primary focus of study on bankruptcy. Along the way, she wrote law review articles across the country, along with academic journal articles, graduating eventually to casebooks, and then books aimed at an academic audience.

As a Harvard law professor, Warren submitted half a dozen briefs to the Supreme Court and began racking up a crowded trophy case of awards for public service and academic study, in addition to the teaching awards she won at the University of Houston, Michigan, and Pennsylvania law schools.

By the time Warren coauthored her first mass-audience nonfiction book, *The Two-Income Trap*, with her daughter Amanda Tyagi Warren in 2004, she had already testified to Congress about bankruptcy three times. From 2005 through 2008 she would appear five more times in front of the House and Senate.

The demand for Professor Warren's expertise in Washington, DC, only grew as she appeared more frequently, until Senate Majority leader Harry Reid (D-NV) appointed[2] her to the Congressional Oversight Panel overseeing President Bush's bank bailout, known as the Troubled Asset Relief Program (TARP).

Two years later, President Obama appointed Warren to serve as an Assistant to the President and special adviser to the Treasury Department, where she designed the Consumer Financial Protection Bureau.

When Senate Republicans indicated that they would not appoint the professor to oversee the federal agency she designed, it had the ironic effect of launching a political career that would send her into their ranks as a colleague just eighteen months later.

Elizabeth Warren didn't have an easy path to victory in Massachusetts over the incumbent, Senator Scott Brown. The Bay State has a 3:1 ratio of Democrats to Republicans, but 52 percent of the electorate that year was not party registered.[3]

Undeterred, Warren ran a bold campaign, and her key statements bled into national politics while she made her first appearance at the Democratic National Convention as a speaker.

In the end, Senator Warren won her first election by a broad mandate, and finished building the policy platform and stellar résumé which propelled her into the 2020 Democratic presidential primary.

WARREN'S CAREER AS AN ACADEMIC AND AUTHOR

During Elizabeth Warren's career as a law professor, she taught three main areas of study; commercial law, contract law and, of course, bankruptcy.

Her courses covered the gamut of banking and business topics including Secured Lending, Empirical Methods, Payment Systems, Commercial Paper, Regulated Industries, Corporations, Partnerships and Banking Regulation.

On college campuses, some professors are well known for their research, but not very interested in teaching. Elizabeth Warren wanted to be a teacher; it was her dream. She won six serious awards for teaching excellence from 1981–1997, one each from Houston Law Center, from University of Michigan (where she only taught for a year as a visiting scholar), one from Harvard University, and three times in her eight years teaching at Penn Law.

Professor Warren's bailiwick is writing, and she has become a prolific author. Her first ever academic journal story was a student work in the *Rutgers Law Review*, covering the topic of Supreme Court decisions in favor of busing students to schools outside their neighborhoods as a tool for desegregating public schools. That was the first of a total of sixty-seven published academic works over thirty-two years. Her work spanned topics from the effect of women in bankruptcy to creating opportunities by linking college to public service opportunities to the changing economics of rearing children. Warren published some of her work in Ivy League law reviews, others with those of large public law schools throughout the Midwest, and many others in the premier journals for bankruptcy law.

Her last academic journal article was easily her most influential. Entitled "Unsafe at Any Rate," it inspired Congress to authorize the Consumer Financial Protection Bureau (CFPB) and for President Obama to appoint her to create the agency.

Three years before she began publishing academic-targeted books and later mass-market books, Warren teamed up with another University of Texas law professor to create a casebook[4] for teaching bankruptcy law entitled *The Law of Debtors and Creditors: Text, Cases, and Problems* which is in its seventh edition.

Since 1989, Warren has authored or coauthored seventeen books, including her most recent offering from 2017, *This Fight Is Our Fight: The*

Battle to Save America's Middle Class. Additionally, she has contributed chapters to eleven other books, many of them about her specialty in bankruptcy law and the larger forces causing more middle-class Americans to seek court protection from their creditors.

She also authored a series of reports on topics ranging from "Financial Difficulties of Small Businesses and Reasons for their Failures" on behalf of the Small Business Administration (SBA) on the reasons homeowners struggle to the declining prospects for America's senior citizens for the AARP's Public Policy Institute in 2008 entitled "Generations of Struggle."

The findings of Warren's report for the AARP, which she coauthored with two sociologists from the University of Michigan and Ohio State University, are likely to find their way into her 2020 presidential candidacy:

> *Debt has become the common denominator of American life. From young people taking on student loans to older Americans struggling to pay for prescription medications, worry over debt has become a constant companion. Last year, more than a million people declared themselves unable to deal with their debts by filing for bankruptcy. Because it is a public manifestation of the most extreme financial trouble, bankruptcy offers one view of the economic health of Americans across the age spectrum.*
>
> *The story from these data is one of rising risk with age. The average age for filing bankruptcy has increased, and the rate of bankruptcy filings among those ages 65 or older has more than doubled since 1991.*

However, it was Elizabeth Warren's books that ultimately impacted her career trajectory the most, beginning with her academic titles according[5] to *Politico Magazine*:

> In the 1980s and '90s, Warren co-wrote two important academic books, As We Forgive Our Debtors *and* The Fragile Middle Class. *Both showed in great detail how the loosening of banking regulations and the shift away from an industrial economy made consumer spending and debt central to middle-class life, and how damaging the effects of this change were to those who simply wanted to hold onto the sort of life that, 30 years before, Warren was raised to believe was expected.*

It was ultimately Warren's writing for the mass market that completely redirected the course of her career[6] from academia into the realm of politics when she published *The Two-Income Trap*. She followed that book up by coauthoring a *New York Times* best-selling personal finance guide, again with her daughter Amelia, entitled *All Your Worth: The Ultimate Lifetime Money Plan*. Her publisher[7] described the central premise of the book this way:

> Warren and Tyagi show you how to balance your money into three essential parts: the Must-Haves (the bills you have to pay every month), the Wants (some fun money for right now), and your Savings (to build a better tomorrow).

A book reviewer at *The Simple Dollar*, a widely read website about personal finance based in Seattle, Washington, summed up *All Your Worth* in a book review[8] thusly:

> There was one key idea that stuck with me from this book, and that was that the real key to personal financial mastery is balance. The first half of the book details a six-step plan for getting your finances in order. In general, the advice is pretty standard, but there are a few interesting twists.

After *All Your Worth* was published, Washington grew exponentially more alluring to the professor over the following seven-year period. It started with frequent trips for Congressional testimony, proceeding to joining and becoming chair of an oversight committee, and then her later executive-branch appointment. Warren's 2012 run for the Senate completed her transition from professor to politician.

WARREN GOES TO WASHINGTON TO TESTIFY, STAYS TO REGULATE

In 2005, Warren testified in person to the Senate Judiciary Committee to oppose the bankruptcy bill—which eventually passed—and continued on to her first time speaking to the committee she would ultimately join in 2013, the Senate's Committee on Banking, Housing, and Urban Affairs. The committee's hearings were entitled "Examining the Billing, Marketing and Disclosure Practices of the Credit Card Industry, and Their Impact on Consumers" and she told[9] the assembled senators on January 25, 2007:

> The credit card market is broken, and consumers pay a steep price in this non-functioning market. But it doesn't have to be this way. I come to you as someone who sees the value in credit cards. I use a credit card—rather frequently. I also believe deeply in the power of free markets.
>
> But today I am here to talk about a market that is not working. . . . Credit card agreements are incomprehensible. They make it impossible for customers to avoid companies that will impose outrageous fees and penalties. The result is a race to adopt practices that will slam consumers the hardest, knowing full well that such behavior will increase company profits dramatically while it costs the card issuers nothing as they recruit new customers.
>
> A growing number of card issuers increase their profits by loading their credit cards with tricks and traps so that they can catch consumers who stumble or mistake those traps for treasure and find themselves caught in a snare from which they cannot escape.

She followed that up four months later with testimony to the Senate Committee on Finance about "The New Economics of the Middle Class: Why Making Ends Meet Has Gotten Harder," and two months after that she testified to the House Judiciary Committee about "Medical Bankruptcy: Middle Class Families at Risk."

Warren testified to Congress for the final time before her appointment to oversee the TARP legislation in March 2008, when she visited the House Committee on Financial Services to speak about "Credit Card Practices That Undermine Consumer Safety."

Seven months after the professor's last visit to Capitol Hill, President Bush signed into law the Emergency Economic Stabilization Act of 2008, which provided $700,000,000,000 to stabilize America's failing investment-banking sector and establishing a Congressional Oversight Panel (COP) to report how TARP funds were used. The act also required that the COP deliver a report to Congress on regulatory reform by January 20, 2009.

After Professor Warren's appointment by the Democratic Senate majority leader on November 14, 2008, she was swiftly elected to chair the panel, a title she held until resigning to take an executive-branch appointment on November 1, 2010. But before then, the COP issued a formal decision[10] based on its thorough audit of the TARP, which confirmed that it indeed was effective in stopping the financial panic caused by years of excessive deregulation in financial markets.

Warren published this message on President Obama's White House website[11] on September 17, 2010, after her appointment[12] to build the CFPB:

The new consumer bureau is based on a pretty simple idea: people ought to be able to read their credit card and mortgage contracts and know the deal. They shouldn't learn about an unfair rule or practice only when it bites them—way too late for them to do anything about it.

The new law creates a chance to put a tough cop on the beat and provide real accountability and oversight of the consumer credit market. The time for hiding tricks and traps in the fine print is over. This new bureau is based on the simple idea that if the playing field is level and families can see what's going on, they will have better tools to make better choices.

"Professor Warren has been a pioneer on the issues before the Consumer Financial Protection Bureau," said[13] Treasury Secretary Timothy Geithner, "and she will now help lead the effort to stand up the agency."

"She was the architect behind the idea for a consumer watchdog," said[14] President Obama that day, "so it only makes sense."

When it came time to appoint a permanent head of the CFBP a year later, Warren's handpicked top enforcement officer, the former Ohio attorney general Richard Codray, got the nod and she embarked on a career in politics soon thereafter.

WARREN'S FIRST POLITICAL CAMPAIGN

On August 18, 2011, Elizabeth Warren launched her senatorial campaign exploratory committee. Early polls[15] showed her trailing the Republican incumbent by more than seven percentage points. The donations poured in to her campaign—though many were from out of state—and she began to stump across the Bay State's fourteen counties. A video from one of those early appearances emerged as one of her central campaign issues[16] in opposition to the Republican Party's tax cuts for the wealthy, when she said:

> You built a factory out there? Good for you. But I want to be clear: you moved your goods to market on the roads the rest of us paid for; you hired workers the rest of us paid to educate; you were safe in your factory because of police forces and fire forces that the rest of us paid for. You didn't have to worry that marauding bands would come and seize everything at your factory, and hire someone to protect against this, because of the work the rest of us did.
>
> Now look, you built a factory and it turned into something terrific, or a great idea? God bless. Keep a big hunk of it. But part of the underlying social contract is you take a hunk of that and pay forward for the next kid who comes along.

In typical Warren fashion, her passionate speech wound up becoming one of the central discussions of the 2012 presidential election, but not for the reasons she intended. President Obama inartfully paraphrased her when he said[17] "you didn't build that" in a moment that both GOP challenger

Mitt Romney and her senatorial opponent would turn into a political attack ad. Washington's *The Hill* newspaper called[18] Brown's attack ad against Warren a "litmus test" for the Republican Party's political arguments that year.

It was a difficult race.

The professor's tough rhetoric didn't enthrall every local pundit, who complained on Boston's NPR station[19] that her advertising campaign was too national "as if she's running for President" and chastised her external characteristics remarking that those matters of style are as politically important as matters of substance.

Early in the campaign, Brown's opposition research uncovered a significant political weakness in Warren's otherwise flawless record. She had self-reported to some, not all of the law schools where she worked and not on her application to Rutgers that based on her family's oral history she was ethnically Native American. Harvard used that information to list her as a minority hire. The AP reported[20] that the school was always interested in the substance of her writing and professional achievements:

> The professor who recruited Warren to Harvard said that any suggestion that she got her job in part because of a claim of minority status is wrong.
>
> "That's totally stupid, ignorant, uninformed and simply wrong," Harvard Law School professor Charles Fried said Monday. "I presented her case to the faculty. I did not mention her Native American connection because I did not know about it."

Independent polling about the senatorial campaign from May 2012 just three weeks after Brown unearthed Warren's claims showed that the voting public did consider her claims to be an important factor in deciding their vote, according to *Politico*:

> *More than two-thirds of voters—69 percent—said Warren's Native American heritage listing is not a significant story, with just 27 percent saying it is. The survey shows the Massachusetts Democrat trailing GOP Sen. Scott Brown by a single percentage point, with Brown netting 48 percent to Warren's 47 percent. The result marks a measurable shift toward Warren since the last Suffolk poll in February, which had Brown up 9 points, 49 percent to 40 percent.*

Three months later, Elizabeth Warren would make her first major splash on the national political stage with a fiery speech to the Democratic National Convention in Charlotte, North Carolina. A key moment of Warren's speech turned out to be a talking point that political leaders on both sides of the aisle would later echo:

> *People feel like the system is rigged against them. And here's the painful part: they're right. The system is rigged.*
> *Look around. Oil companies guzzle down billions in subsidies. Billionaires pay lower tax rates than their secretaries. Wall Street CEOs—the same ones who wrecked*

our economy and destroyed millions of jobs—still strut around Congress, no shame, demanding favors, and acting like we should thank them. Anyone here have a problem with that? Well I do.

The Atlantic called[21] Warren one of "only two speakers during the pre-Clinton part of the evening to put some fire into the crowd." Her perceptive turn of phrase that the "system is rigged," which is based upon decades of empirical research, will long outlive her 2012 senatorial campaign in American politics.

After a lengthy campaign, Massachusetts voters went to the polls in November 2012 and elected Elizabeth Warren to be their new senator. Of the ten polls that *Huffington Post* tracked,[22] only one of them accurately predicted that she would prevail with 53 percent of the vote and it happened to be by Suffolk University, the same pollster who said that voters care more about the issues than the political sideshows her opponent presented.

Poll	Warren	Brown	Undecided	Spread
UMass Lowell/Herald Oct 31 – Nov 3, 2012 800 Likely Voters	48	**49**	2	Brown +1
YouGov Oct 31 – Nov 3, 2012 811 Likely Voters	**50**	43	7	Warren +7
PPP (D) Nov 1 – Nov 2, 2012 1,089 Likely Voters	**52**	46	2	Warren +6
Kimball Political Consulting (R) Oct 31 – Nov 1, 2012 761 Likely Voters	47	**49**	5	Brown +2
WNEU/MassLive.com Oct 26 – Nov 1, 2012 535 Likely Voters	**50**	46	–	Warren +4
Suffolk Oct 25 – Oct 28, 2012 600 Likely Voters	**53**	46	1	Warren +7
Boston Globe/UNH Oct 24 – Oct 28, 2012 583 Likely Voters	**47**	**47**	–	
Rasmussen Oct 25 – Oct 25, 2012 500 Likely Voters	**52**	47	–	Warren +5
MassINC/WBUR Oct 21 – Oct 22, 2012 516 Likely Voters	**50**	44	6	Warren +6
Kimball Political Consulting (R) Oct 18 – Oct 21, 2012 761 Likely Voters	**48**	46	7	Warren +2

Senator-elect Warren's statements about the importance of the commonwealth provided by governments did wind up being a litmus test for American politics in 2012, and it appears to be one of the more important reasons why voters chose her over the incumbent and reelected President Barack Obama during that year's general election.

Two years later she published her memoir, entitled *A Fighting Chance,* which[23] the *New York Times* called "a potent mix of memoir and policy that makes politics seem like a necessary evil, and yet it's impossible to read Warren's story without thinking about her meteoric rise in the Democratic Party and those Warren groupies on Connecticut Avenue."

Her most recent book, *This Fight Is Our Fight: The Battle to Save America's Middle Class,* was published in April 2017. It's a stirring political call to action in the new American political climate.

On January 3, 2013, Massachusetts Senator John Kerry escorted Elizabeth Warren to the well of the Senate, where then–Vice President Joe Biden swore her into office. Twenty-seven days later, Kerry resigned to serve as President Obama's Secretary of State, and she became the state's senior senator.

Senator Warren immediately began serving on three committees[1] which suited her talents and experience in the law and finance, on which she still sits today: the Committee on Health, Education, Labor, and Pensions (HELP), the Special Committee on Aging, and the Committee on Banking, Housing, and Urban Affairs. In 2015, she joined the Committee on Energy and Natural Resources, but switched to the Committee on Armed Services in 2017, which she sits on today. Warren's total of four committee assignments is typical for the Senate.

Warren's role in the Committee on Banking, Housing, and Urban Affairs has attracted the most public attention, and her public profile has only grown in recent years because she's not afraid to grill the heads of large banks. Just googling the term "Warren grills bank CEO" quickly reveals her dogged oversight of Wells Fargo Bank.

A RAPID RISE TO SENATE LEADERSHIP

Senator Warren has spent four of her six years in Congress with divided partisan leadership and the other two years under a GOP-controlled Senate and House. Yet, she has managed to consistently introduce and sometimes pass bipartisan legislation, even with Donald Trump in the White House. Freshman senators aren't known for passing a lot of legislation in a body that prizes seniority, but Warren bucked the trend after Minority leader Harry Reid (D-NV) appointed her to a leadership position in the Democratic Senate conference after the 2014 midterm elections.

Reid created the special role just for Warren[2] that gave her a voice in shaping policy and communications for the conference as an envoy to the liberal wing of the party. "Wall Street is doing very well, CEOs are bringing in millions more and families all across this country are struggling," she said after the vote, according[3] to CNN. "We have to make this government work for the American people."

Two years later, after another disappointing election, Reid invited Warren to his office just before Thanksgiving 2016. He told her then that she needed to think seriously about running for president in 2020. Forty days later, Harry Reid left the senate after thirty years, the last twelve of them leading the Democratic caucus.

"He was worried in November," Warren told[4] the *New York Times Magazine* about her fateful meeting with Reid. "For me, it was so important to make clear: We will fight back—we will fight back. We're not here to make this normal."

Today, Warren is serving[5] as one of the Democratic Senate conference's two vice chairs along with Sen. Mark Warner (D-VA).

CONSUMER ADVOCACY TAKES CENTER STAGE

The Consumer Financial Protection Bureau (CFPB)—which Warren designed—caught Wells Fargo creating millions of fake accounts. Regulators fined the large bank a total of $185,000,000,[6] and its CEO, John G. Stumpf, testified in front of the Banking Committee. Senator Warren's scalding commentary on September 20, 2016, made national headlines when she told Stumpf to resign. But she made a larger point about the lack of accountability atop America's largest banks. She said:[7]

> *If one of your tellers took a handful of $20 bills out of the cash drawer, they'd probably be looking at criminal charges for theft; they could end up in prison. But you squeezed your employees to the breaking point so they would cheat customers and you could drive up the value of your stock and put hundreds of millions of dollars in your own pocket. And when it all blew up, you kept your job, you kept your multimillion dollar bonuses, and you went on television to blame thousands of $12 an hour employees who were just trying to make cross sell quotas to make you rich.*
>
> *You should resign. You should give back the money that you took while this scam was going on and you should be criminally investigated.*

A week later Wells Fargo announced that its CEO would forfeit $41 million in stock awards, and, two weeks after that, John G. Stumpf resigned in disgrace as both CEO and chairman of the board.[8]

In 2018, the CFPB caught Wells Fargo cheating its mortgage customers and fined it a billion dollars.[9] Another report into Wells Fargo's collegiate banking services found that they charge an average of quadruple the fees of the largest provider of services to college students and the highest out of 573 banks on all American college campuses. That led Senator Warren to call for Wells Fargo to be removed from colleges across the country after the report was released in late 2018.[10]

"When granted the privilege of providing financial services to students through colleges, Wells Fargo used this access to charge struggling college students exorbitant fees," Warren said.[11] "These high fees, which are an outlier within the industry, demonstrate conclusively that Wells Fargo does not belong on college campuses."

WARREN'S ROLE IN THE RISE OF THE RESISTANCE

As a senator, Senator Warren has never been afraid to respectfully challenge her colleagues, even if that means occasionally having to stand up to the Democratic caucus. But her opposition to President Trump and his Republican allies in the Senate after the 2016 election led to a new rallying cry for women across America who refuse to be silenced. Senator Warren's early leadership in the Resistance helped spark a mass political movement that flipped most recent seats in the House of Representatives in 2018, returning it to Democratic control.

First, she led an impromptu rally at Boston's Logan Airport a day after Trump enacted a surprise executive order banning Muslims from entering the America on Saturday, January 28, barely a week after his inauguration.

"We will make our voices heard all around this world. We have all heard about this order that President Trump has given. It is illegal. It is unconstitutional. And it will be overturned," said Warren[12] while holding a bullhorn, but speaking without it. "An attack on anyone for their religious beliefs is an attack on the very foundation of democracy."

Then, when Trump nominated former Alabama Senator Jeff Sessions to be the new Attorney General, Senator Warren strongly disagreed with his confirmation and spoke out. Senators tend to be extremely deferential to their colleagues, which led to a high-profile confrontation with Republican leadership. Sessions had been previously denied an appointment to the federal bench in 1986 by a Republican-controlled Senate Judiciary Committee after a former employee blew the whistle on his open racism. "In doing so, that Senate affirmed that there can be no compromise with racism; no negotiation with hate," Warren told Bloomberg News' Sahil Kapur[13] about the Sessions nomination.

Sahil Kapur ✓
@sahilkapur

Following ∨

Elizabeth Warren says a Sessions AG nom means Trump is "embracing the bigotry that fueled his campaign rallies."

~~Donald Trump plans to nominate Senator Jeff~~ Sessions to serve as U.S. Attorney General:

"Instead of embracing the bigotry that fueled his campaign rallies, I urge President-elect Trump to reverse his apparent decision to nominate Senator Sessions to be Attorney General of the United States. If he refuses, then it will fall to the Senate to exercise fundamental moral leadership for our nation and all of its people. Thirty years ago, a different Republican Senate rejected Senator Sessions' nomination to a federal judgeship. In doing so, that Senate affirmed that there can be no compromise with racism; no negotiation with hate. Today, a new Republican Senate must

2:33 PM - 18 Nov 2016

208 Retweets **206** Likes

💬 30   ↻ 208   ≋   ♡ 206   ✉

During the hearings, that's when Senator Warren began to read a letter from Dr. Martin Luther King Jr.'s wife Coretta Scott King, which her longtime predecessor Sen. Edward Kennedy (D-MA) had submitted to the Senate during Sessions' failed confirmation hearing. King wrote an impassioned plea to keep Sessions off the bench over his racially biased use of his office as the U.S. Attorney for Southern Alabama. The key part of her letter reads:

> *Civil rights leaders, including my husband and Albert Turner, have fought long and hard to achieve free and unfettered access to the ballot box. Mr. SESSIONS has used the awesome power of his office to chill the free exercise of the vote by black citizens in the district he now seeks to serve as a federal judge. This simply cannot be allowed to happen. Mr. SESSIONS' conduct as U.S. Attorney, from his politically-motivated voting fraud prosecutions to his indifference toward criminal violations of civil rights laws, indicates that he lacks the temperament, fairness and judgment to be a federal judge.*

That's when Senate Majority leader Mitch McConnell (R-KY) interrupted Warren, claiming that reading King's letter into the record violated Senate Rule XIX that proscribes disparaging the motives of another senator, since Sessions kept his seat during the confirmation hearings.

"I am surprised that the words of Coretta Scott King are not suitable for debate in the United States Senate. I ask leave of the Senate to continue my remarks," Senator Warren told the Montana senator presiding over the hearing. Again, McConnell objected. The Senate voted to end Warren's speech along party lines 49–43.

It was the Republican majority leader's smarmy remarks after that vote that became an ironic and iconic rallying cry for women of the Resistance:

> *Senator Warren was giving a lengthy speech. She had appeared to violate the rule.*
>
> *She was warned. She was given an explanation.*
> *Nevertheless, she persisted.*

"Some called it a gift to women's rights," wrote[14] the *New York Times* as the incident went viral on Twitter, "and the episode angered many who diagnosed it as a plot to muzzle a vocal senator, Elizabeth Warren, Democrat of Massachusetts."

"By silencing Elizabeth Warren," California senator and 2020 Democratic primary candidate Kamala Harris tweeted[15] that day, "the GOP gave women around the world a rallying cry."

 **Kamala Harris**
@KamalaHarris

By silencing Elizabeth Warren, the GOP gave women around the world a rallying cry. #ShePersisted #LetLizSpeak

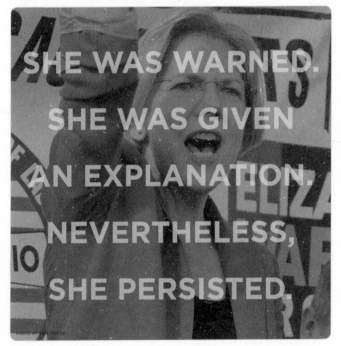

SHE WAS WARNED.

SHE WAS GIVEN

AN EXPLANATION.

NEVERTHELESS,

SHE PERSISTED.

12:19 PM - 8 Feb 2017

17,356 Retweets **33,770** Likes

♡ 729　⟲ 17K　❤ 34K

PASSING BIPARTISAN LEGISLATION

Senator Warren has not been able to pass any sweeping legislation during the last six years of divided government. However, she has found common ground with her conservative counterparts in the Senate to propose and sometimes even pass consensus initiatives.

Barely one month after her rise to Democratic leadership at the end of 2014, the Senate unanimously passed a bill she cosponsored with Sen. Rob Portman (R-OH) called the Smart Savings Act.[16] The bill changed the way that federal employees retirement savings works in order to maximize the return to workers who save.

Two years later, she cosponsored a bill to combat the prescription opioid crisis called the Reducing Unused Medications Act that allowed patients to buy less than the fully prescribed doses of painkillers. It became law[17] in 2016 as part of a broader bill, which led Massachusetts Medical Society President James S. Gessner, MD to say:

> We applaud and thank Senator Warren and Congress-woman Clark for their support and leadership on fighting the opioid epidemic. The ability of physicians to write partial-fill prescriptions will help to reduce the amount of unused pain medicines, thereby limiting the number of drugs that can be diverted.

Even though she began leading the political resistance to President Trump's policies in 2017, that's also when Senator Warren significantly increased her bipartisan bill output with her Republican colleagues.

It started when Warren cosponsored a bill with Sen. Chuck Grassley (R-IA) to make hearing aids available over the counter, which passed[18] by a 94–1 vote as part of a broader package. Only Senator Bernie Sanders (I-VT)—who also sits on the HELP Committee—voted against the broader bill.[19] Sanders considered the bill (which was necessary to fund the Food and Drug Adminsitration (FDA)) a "giveaway to the pharmaceutical industry" and said that it didn't bring down drug prices after his amendment to allow Americans to more easily obtain medications from Canada was rejected.

The AARP reported[20] that prescription hearing aids for those with moderate hearing loss averaged $2,400 per person, while nonprescription aids that Warren's bill makes available cost only $500 each.

"Everyone leaned forward and said this is the kind of change that will help bring down health care costs in America," Warren said in an exclusive interview[21] with *Politico* after passing the bill. "Forty-eight million Americans have hearing loss, but fewer than one in six gets a hearing aid that could help them and the principal reason is because they can't afford it."

The senior Massachusetts senator also became the primary Democratic cosponsor of the Jobs for Our Heroes Act, a bill with Sen. Thom Tillis (R-NC) and Sen. John Cornyn (R-TX) who is the majority whip and top deputy to leader McConnell. That bill passed the Senate with unanimous consent,[22] and makes it easier for veterans to obtain Commercial Driver's Licenses when they leave military service. President Trump signed it into law in early 2018.

"Now that this bill has been signed into law, veterans will be able to more easily transfer the commercial driving skills they've honed in the military to civilian life, and therefore more easily find jobs that pair well with their skillset," the GOP senator Cornyn told[23] the Fayetteville (NC) *Observer.*

Senators Warren and Cornyn didn't wait long to propose more legislation either. The same day that their first bill became law on January 8, 2018, the senators introduced[24] the Bankruptcy Venue Reform Act together. As a Harvard professor, she opposed a Republican-backed bankruptcy bill, and now, she found common ground to try and end a loophole that allowed large corporations to venue-shop when they file bankruptcy, in order to seek maximum advantage or lenient judges.

"Workers, creditors, and consumers lose when corporations manipulate the system to file for bankruptcy wherever they please," said Sen. Warren about the bill her Republican colleague promised would restore integrity to the bankruptcy court system. "I'm glad to work with Senator Cornyn to prevent big companies from cherry-picking courts that they think will rule in their favor and to crack down on this corporate abuse of our nation's bankruptcy laws."

Unfortunately, Warren's bankruptcy reform bill didn't gain traction in the Senate and become law, nor did the STATES Act, which was her effort to delegate marijuana laws cosponsored with Sen. Cory Gardner (R-CO) in 2018.[25]

Bloomberg TV ✔
@BloombergTV

Follow ∨

Senator Cory Gardner (R-CO) discusses his bill that would allow banking for the marijuana industry
bloom.bg/2QSS7z5

Sen. Cory Gardner
■(R) COLORADO

Bloomberg · SEN. GARDNER ON MARIJUANA AMENDMENT TO CRIMINAL JUSTICE REFORM BILL

Sen. Gardner on Marijuana Banking

10:36 AM - 17 Dec 2018

3 Retweets 8 Likes

An independent analysis of the bills that Senator Warren sponsored and cosponsored from 2015 through 2019 by the independent political website GovTrack.us[26] rates her as tied for the thirteenth most liberal member of the senate. In comparison, her opponents in the 2020 Democratic primary are Sen. Amy Klobuchar (D-MN), who is rated the thirty-fourth most liberal senator, then Sen. Cory Booker (D-NJ) is ranked seventeenth most liberal, Sen. Harris is ranked fourth most liberal, Sen. Sanders is ranked second most liberal, and Sen. Kirsten Gillibrand (D-NY) is ranked the most liberal, member of the Senate.

GovTrack's proprietary leadership rankings based upon how many bills she sponsored or cosponsored ranked her thirteenth out of her forty-seven Democratic colleagues for leadership. Their scorecard[27] of Warren's activity in the 115th Congress from 2017–2019 reveals that more than half of the eighty bills she submitted had bipartisan sponsors. Five of the bills she wrote became law, including the three bills noted above and a measure impacting Veterans Affairs educational requirements and bill directing the U.S. Treasury to mint a coin commemorating the Naismith Memorial Basketball Hall of Fame in her home state.

Warren's bills had the ninth most support of all senators in the House with twenty-two of her eighty bills sponsored in the lower chamber, and thirteen of her bills got voted out of committee and received floor votes.

Senator Warren did not miss a single vote out of the 599 votes in the 115th Congress, even while running for reelection and preparing her present presidential run.

2018 REELECTION CAMPAIGN

Before the Warren for President campaign could launch, the senator still had one very important task without which her 2020 aspirations would mean nothing; securing her reelection. For the second time in her two races, she didn't face a Democratic primary opponent for the nomination.

Unlike her first campaign in 2012 against the incumbent Senator Scott Brown (R-MA) when the nonpartisan Cook Report rated the race a toss-up, Warren's second campaign never appeared to be seriously in doubt. She faced two challengers, Mass. State Rep. Geoff Diehl (R-Plymouth) and MIT-educated scientist Shiva Ayyadurai, who left the Republican primary to run as an independent.

State Rep. Diehl handily beat three other candidates in the Republican primary, winning a majority in thirteen out of fourteen counties in Massachusetts. Diehl's major claims to fame were supporting a successful gas tax initiative in 2014 and his position as a cochair of the 2016 Trump campaign in the Bay State. A lengthy investigation[28] by Boston's local NPR radio station WGBH was unable to prove that Diehl actually did anything for the Trump campaign. Hillary Clinton won an overwhelming 60.1 percent of the state's vote in the 2016 race and Warren would virtually replicate her performance, improving on her margins from 2012.

The Associated Press called the race[29] in favor of Senator Warren at 8 p.m. on election night, immediately after the polls closed and before the votes were tallied. When the dust settled, she won 60.3 percent of the votes,[30] including thirteen out of fourteen counties in Massachusetts, except in Plymouth, which is Diehl's home county. Warren outperformed every major poll in the race. Diehl won 36.2 percent of the vote and the independent candidate underperformed most of the polls, named on only 3.4 percent of the ballots cast. Warren gave a victory speech[31] to her supporters, saying:

> When I first ran for the Senate six years ago, I asked you
> to take a chance on someone who had never even run for

office before. You took that chance. You sent me into the fight. And tonight you told me to stay in the fight. I'm deeply grateful, and I promise I will never stop working my heart out for you—never.

It's been a tough two years. But together, we have marched. Together, we have run. Together, we have persisted . . . and insisted that our voices be heard, that our votes be counted, and that our values be respected.

It would be weeks after election night before Warren's meeting with outgoing Senate minority leader Reid, who urged her to prepare a presidential run, but it was no secret that she already had big aspirations.

"Elizabeth Warren Wins. She's Still Your Senator, For Now," read the headline[32] in *Boston Magazine*, which was subtitled, "She brushed off a challenge from Geoff Diehl. Now what?"

PREPARING HER RUN FOR PRESIDENT

Senator Warren announced her presidential exploratory committee on December 31, 2018, and officially entered the race on February 9, 2019. For her supporters, it was the culmination of a four-year effort to "Draft Warren" to run for president, which began[33] before the 2014 midterm elections with a group of Obama supporters.[34] Eighteen months after Sen. Reid's encouragement to run for president, Warren released a series of sweeping bills that make up the bulk of her campaign's domestic policy agenda.

Senator Warren filed the following bills from March 2018 to March 2019, which are relevant to her campaign:

- The Anti-Corruption and Public Integrity Act to reform lobbying and strengthen ethics laws
- The American Housing and Economic Mobility Act, which is a jobs bill that would lower rents for workforce housing
- The Climate Risk Disclosure Act would require America's public companies to disclose their climate-change risks and exposure
- The Accountable Capitalism Act would require worker participation on corporate boards and new checks against large corporations who commit crimes

She also cosponsored her opponent Senator Harris's Medicare for All bill in February 2019, which would provide a "public option" as a means to strive toward universal health insurance coverage.

It's not unusual for a senator who is preparing a presidential campaign to attract significant criticism for taking too much time away from their duties to prepare a national campaign. In contrast, when the *Boston Globe,* her hometown newspaper, picked through[35] Senator Warren's schedules and travel history, they discovered that she had spent 74 percent of her time in either Massachusetts or Washington doing her job and hasn't missed a Senate vote in years. They also determined that she held thirty-seven town halls from the start of 2017 through the 2018 midterm election, which she took note to tell viewers during her first 2020 campaign nationally televised town hall on CNN.

ANALYSIS: WARREN'S CHANCES FOR WINNING THE NOMINATION AND PRESIDENCY

Elizabeth Warren launched her 2020 presidential exploratory committee first among the top-tier Democrats in the primary, but she's embraced the early underdog role thus far, devoting a significant amount of time to early voting states like New Hampshire, Iowa, South Carolina, and Nevada. She has hired sixty-five staffers as of mid-March 2019.[1]

The Warren campaign is staked on the senator's carefully planned and analyzed domestic proposals. Her decision to eschew certain elements of typical high-dollar campaigns hurts her measurable statistics in the short term compared to her competitors, but shouldn't hurt her long-term prospects which will likely be shaped by the primary debates.

Early polling shows that Senator Warren's tax plan is a bipartisan hit,[2] with 60 percent approval of those surveyed in a *Politico*/Morning Consult poll conducted in February 2019. Amazingly, her "ultra wealth tax" has

50 percent approval among Republican voters, along with 56 percent of independents and 75 percent of Democrats.

"By running a very intimate and grass roots campaign, with town halls and small events, she's perfecting her knowledge and understanding of the concerns and issues of voters," says Fernand Amandi, who runs the polling firm Bendixen & Amandi International, in an interview about Warren's early candidacy. "There's no better way to understand what they want. If she can translate that to amazing debate performances that might propel her into the top tier and engage a real grassroots fundraising base."

"I know that the way I've decided to run my campaign means that I'm leaving millions of dollars on the table," Warren told the AP in March. "This is about meeting people in person. Talking with them about the things that touch their lives every day, about their hopes to make this country work not just for the rich and the powerful, but to make it work for them."

Very early polling showed Warren polling sixth out of a vast universe of twenty-eight candidates, but at the early stage of the campaign most of the people polled were undecided.

However, "polls this far out don't really mean a whole lot, but they do show a snapshot of the temperature of the electorate at this moment in time," says Amandi, who is a regular contributor to MSNBC's weekend program *AM Joy*. "She certainly doesn't start out in the top tier of candidates for the nomination. I think her unorthodox approach where she forgoes raising big dollars that allow her to put in place an infrastructure for the long haul, it's a risk. That said, she's running a very technically sound campaign, with a clearly articulated message that defines well what her candidacy is about."

Early state polling reveals an interesting dynamic with Warren in neighboring New Hampshire, where she was the choice of 17 percent surveyed Democrats in a University of New Hampshire poll before the rest of the field declared, and about 7 percent of today's voter samples. However, only one out of twenty New Hampshire Democrats is decided according[3] to CNN. The Real Clear Politics composite poll[4] puts Warren at 8.3 percent support of the surveyed voters.

A recent Emerson poll[5] in Iowa placed Warren at 9 percent support behind Harris and surprising newcomer, South Bend, Indiana's Mayor Pete Buttigieg, then Sanders and Biden. Another Emerson poll in Wisconsin[6] surveyed a hypothetical presidential election between several of the front-running Democratic candidates found a Warren/Trump matchup siding in favor of the senator by 4 percent. A contemporaneous Fox News poll[7] shows the opposite, with Warren trailing Trump by 2 percent in a hypothetical matchup from a poll indicating a 51 percent disapproval rating for the president.

A poll conducted in Florida by Bendixen & Amandi showed that Senator Warren is in fourth place with 4 percent support as of March 2019.

There will be a Democratic Presidential Primary election in Florida on March 17th 2020 to determine the Democratic Party nominee for President. For whom would you vote if the election were held today and the candidates were:Joe Biden, Michael Bloomberg, Cory Booker, Sherrod Brown, Pete Buttigieg, Julian Castro, John Delaney, Kirsten Gillibrand, Tulsi Gabbard, Kamala Harris, John Hickenlooper, Jay Inslee, Amy Klobuchar, Beto O'Rourke, Bernie Sanders, Elizabeth Warren or Andrew Yang?

BY AGE

	18-49	50-64	65+
Joe Biden	32%	25%	17%
Bernie Sanders	13%	11%	10%
Kamala Harris	9%	13%	6%
Elizabeth Warren	2%	6%	4%
Cory Booker	1%	3%	-
Undecided	44%	41%	55%

BENDIXEN & AMANDI
INTERNATIONAL

28 WWW.BENDIXENANDAMANDI.COM A SURVEY OF FLORIDA VOTERS ONE YEAR BEFORE THE PRESIDENTIAL PRIMARY – MARCH 2019

"Right now, her poll numbers in Florida are within the margin of error, but she sits in the middle of the pack in such a large field," says Amandi about his firm's polling results. "A year out, she's well behind the top three finishers, Joe Biden, Bernie Sanders, and Kamala Harris, in that order. Forty-six percent of the poll participants were undecided in our March 2019 Florida poll, which exceeds the top candidate by twenty points."

Ultimately, Warren is probably counting on pairing her grassroots campaign with earned media, and it's not an unsound strategy considering that she has such an extensive set of proposals while nine of her opponents didn't have a single policy idea on their websites[8] as of March 22, 2019.

Her campaign advisers have already told the AP that she plans to introduce new initiatives "in real time," like she did with a proposal to break up or regulate America's largest tech companies. It means that she could potentially catch the national zeitgeist and take off, or if she has a ridiculed idea it could sink her campaign.

"There's an interesting element to what Elizabeth Warren's doing. It's high risk, but very high reward," says the pollster Amandi. "I think the debates in the Democratic primary will be as decisive as they were in the Republican primary in 2016. When you have this many candidates, many of whom are aligned on the issues, the debates will go a long way toward separating the pack."

"I kept telling people: 'Just wait. Wait and watch,' Warren backer Rep. Joe Kennedy III told the AP, arguing that she has proven doubters wrong since the start of her political career.

The 2020 Democratic primary race will go on for thirteen months before the first votes are cast in New Hampshire's primary some time before February 11, 2020. That means we will see a lot of dynamic changes in voter preferences as events unfold and some of the 95 percent voters who are undecided begin to settle on their choices.

Elizabeth Warren's popular early policy proposals demonstrate that she definitely has the potential to surprise both her detractors and pundits to the upside. All that remains to be seen is if her high-risk strategy yields rewards, or if it peters out when voters head to the polls.

Early polling of the head-to-head matchup between Warren and the president indicates that she should have the capacity to beat Donald Trump.

It's difficult to analyze her chances of winning the nomination, because the race is so crowded at the time of writing in late March 2019, but it is safe to say that because of her extensive domestic policy experience, she will be highly sought as a running mate if she doesn't win the primary.

Elizabeth Warren can win the Democratic nomination. Candidates with far less experience and fewer policy ideas have made their way out of the Democratic primary in the past. Her educational background, writing skills, and speaking skills make her a threat to break out of the middle of the pack when debate season begins in summer 2019.

BIBLIOGRAPHY

CHAPTER 1

1. DeCosta-Klipa, Nick. "3 must-watch moments from the Elizabeth Warren-Geoff Diehl debate." October 20, 2018. Boston.com.

CHAPTER 2

1. Oberman, Mira. "Obama Surprise Visit Sparks Pandemonium At Graduation." June 11, 2018. Agence France-Presse.
2. Warren, Elizabeth. "Unsafe at Any Rate." *Democracy Journal.* Issue 5, Summer 2007.
3. "Remarks by the President at a Campaign Event." July 6, 2012. Whitehouse.gov.
4. Bland, Scott. "Warren Raised $299K Online on Launch Day of Exploratory Committee." February 1, 2019. *Politico.*

Dovere, Edward-Isaac, Matthew Nussbaum, Annie Karni, and Daniel Strauss. "Sanders Had Big Ideas but Little Impact on Capitol Hill." *Politico.* March 12, 2016.

5. McGrane, Victoria. "Five Things to Know About Elizabeth Warren's Record in the US Senate." November 2, 2018. *Boston Globe.* Bostonglobe.com.

CHAPTER 3

1. Jacobs, Samuel P. "Elizabeth Warren: 'I Created Occupy Wall Street.'" October 25, 2011. *The Daily Beast*.

2. "Hearing Before the Committee on the Judiciary United States Senate." February 10, 2005. Govinfo.gov.

3. Ibid.

4. Congressional Oversight Panel, February Oversight Report, February 6, 2005. Govinfo.gov.

5. *The Early Show*. "Elizabeth Warren discusses why so many two-income families are having financial problems." Hannah Storm. CBS News. September 10, 2003, air date via Nexis.com.

6. *American Morning*. "Going Broke." Bill Hemmer. CNN. September 16, 2003, air date via Nexis.com.

7. Warren, Elizabeth, and Amelia Warren Tyagi. 2007. *The Two-Income Trap*. New York: Basic Books.

8. Office of Senator Chuck Grassley. "Opening Statement of Sen. Chuck Grassley at the Bankruptcy Reform Hearing | Chuck Grassley." February 10, 2005. Grassley.Senate.gov.

9. Hayashi, Yuka. "At Consumer Finance Agency, a Critic Is Now the One Pulling the Levers." October 21, 2018. *Wall Street Journal*.

10. "Toward a 21st Century Approach to Consumer Protection | Consumer Financial Protection Bureau." November 15, 2018. Consumer Financial Protection Bureau.

11. "President Barack Obama and Secretary Geithner Escort Elizabeth Warren." September 17, 2010. The White House.

12. "President Obama Names Elizabeth Warren Assistant to the President and Special Advisor to the Secretary of the Treasury on the Consumer Financial Protection Bureau." September 17, 2010. Whitehouse.gov.

13. Corn, David. "Elizabeth Warren: Passed Over For CFPB Post, But . . ." July 18, 2011. *Mother Jones.*

14. Huey-Burns, Caitlin. "Elizabeth Warren Launches Exploratory Committee." August 18, 2011. Realclearpolitics.com.

15. Mystal, Elie, Legal Network, and Katherine Recruiting. "Female Law Professors Continue Their Assault on the World." September 14, 2011. *Above the Law.*

16. "The Economic Platform and Promises of Candidate Barack Obama in 2008." February 10, 2019. *The Balance.*

17. Siders, David, and Caitlin Oprysko. "Despite Crowds, Beto Campaign Gets A Rocky Rollout." March 18, 2019. *Politico.*

18. Lee, MJ, and Donie O'Sullivan, CNN. "Elizabeth Warren's Mission to Break Up Facebook Gets Help—From Facebook." March 12, 2019. CNN.

CHAPTER 4

1. Conniff, Ruth. "And They're Off! Candidates Race to Challenge Trump in 2020." November 15, 2018. *The Progressive.*

2. Clinton, Hillary. "The 100 Most Influential People: Elizabeth Warren." April 15, 2015. *Time.*

3. Warren, Elizabeth. "Opinion | Companies Shouldn't be Accountable Only to Shareholders." August 14, 2018. *Wall Street Journal.*

4. "Text - S.3357 - 115th Congress (2017–2018): Anti-Corruption and Public Integrity Act." August 21, 2018. Congress.gov. https://www.congress.gov/bill/115th-congress/senate-bill/3357/text.

5. Warmbrodt, Zachary. "Warren Proposes Sweeping Crackdown on Lobbying." August 21, 2018. *Politico.*

6. Office of Senator Elizabeth Warren. "Anti-Corruption Act summary." August 21, 2018. Warren.Senate.gov. https://www.warren.senate.gov/imo/media/doc/2018.08.21%20Anti%20Corruption%20Act%20Summary.pdf.

7. "Revolving Door Summary: Former Members." Opensecrets.org. https://www.opensecrets.org/revolving/top.php?display=Z. Accessed March 26, 2019.

8. "Federal Court: Media Basics—Journalist's Guide." Accessed March 27, 2016. United States Courts. https://www.uscourts.gov/statistics-reports/federal-court-media-basics-journalists-guide.

9. "All Info - S.65 - 115th Congress (2017–2018): Presidential Conflicts of Interest Act of 2017." January 9, 2017. Congress.gov. https://www.congress.gov/bill/115th-congress/senate-bill/65/all-info.

10. Media Release. "Warren's Legislation Would Peel Away Layers of Corruption Statement of Robert Weissman, President, Public Citizen." August 21, 2018. https://www.citizen.org/media/press-releases/warren%E2%80%99s-legislation-would-peel-away-layers-corruption.

11. Office of Senator Elizabeth Warren. "Warren Anti-Corruption Bill Gains Momentum as Jayapal, Sarbanes, Others Co-Sponsor House

Companion | U.S. Senator Elizabeth Warren Of Massachusetts."
November 26, 2018. Warren.Senate.gov.

12. Warren, Elizabeth. "Ultra-Millionaire Tax | Elizabeth Warren."
    January 24, 2019. *Warren for President*. https://elizabethwarren.com
    /ultra-millionaire-tax/.

13. "Understanding Taxes—Theme 3: Fairness in Taxes—Lesson 3:
    Progressive Taxes." Accessed March 24, 2019. IRS. https://apps.irs
    .gov/app/understandingTaxes/student/whys_thm03_les03.jsp.

14. Saez, Emmanuel, and Gabriel Zucman. "Letter to Elizabeth Warren
    regarding your proposal to impose a progressive annual wealth tax."
    January 18, 2019. UC, Berkeley. http://bit.ly/2FrgIEs.

15. Warren, Elizabeth. "My Plan For Universal Child Care." February
    19, 2019. *Medium*. https://medium.com/@teamwarren/my-plan-for
    -universal-child-care-762535e6c20a.

16. Geman, Ben. "Elizabeth Warren Backs The "Idea" of a Green New
    Deal." January 1, 2019. *Axios*.

17. Ibid.

18. "Best Countries for Raising Kids." February 5, 2018. *U.S. News &
    World Report*.

19. Astor, Maggie. "Elizabeth Warren Proposes Universal Child Care."
    February 19, 2019. *New York Times*.

20. "Poverty Guidelines." February 1, 2019. U.S. Dept. of Health and
    Human Services. https://aspe.hhs.gov/poverty-guidelines.

21. "Head Start (Program)." Accessed March 25, 2019. Wikipedia.
    https://en.wikipedia.org/wiki/Head_Start_(program).

22. Zandi, Mark, and Sophia Koropeckyj. "Universal Child Care and Early Learning Act: Helping Families and the Economy." February 2, 2019. Economy.com/*Moody's Analytics.*

23. Office of Senator Elizabeth Warren. "Universal Child Care and Early Learning Act Brief." February 18, 2019. Warren.Senate.gov.

24. Tapper, Jake. "CNN Hosts Town Hall with Sen. Elizabeth Warren (D-MA)." March 18th, 2019. CNN.

25. Warren, Elizabeth. "My Housing Plan for America." March 16, 2019. *Medium.* https://medium.com/@teamwarren/my-housing-plan-for-america-20038e19dc26.

26. Zandi, Mark, and Sophia Koropeckyj. "Addressing the Affordable Housing Crisis." September 28, 2018. Economy.com/*Moody's Analytics.*

27. Ibid.

28. Capital Magnet Fund. "Solutions for Affordable Housing in Low-Income Communities." May 12, 2017.

29. Baradaran, Mehrsa, and Darrick Hamilton. "Elizabeth Warren's New Housing Proposal Is Actually a Brilliant Plan to Close the Racial Wealth Gap." October 26, 2018. *Slate.*

30. "Definition of redlining." Accessed March 28, 2019. Merriam-Webster.com.

31. Warren, Elizabeth. "Here's How We Can Break Up Big Tech." March 8, 2019. *Medium.*

32. Stern, Grant. "Facebook Just Got Caught Censoring Elizabeth Warren for Her Policies." March 11, 2019. *Washington Press.*

33. Warren, Elizabeth. "Curious why I think FB has too much power? Let's start with their ability to shut down a debate over whether FB has too much power. Thanks for restoring my posts. But I want a social media marketplace that isn't dominated by a single censor. #BreakUpBigTech." Quotes other Tweet. March 11, 2019. 7:59 p.m. https://twitter.com/ewarren/status/1105256905058979841.

34. "Text - H.R.1 - 116th Congress (2019–2020): For the People Act of 2019." March 12, 2019. Congress.gov.

35. Robinson, Karl. "A Look at the Impact of Citizens United on Its 9th Anniversary." *Opensecrets News*. January 21, 2019.

36. Corrigan, Jack, Government Executive. "The Hollowing Out of the State Department Continues." February 11, 2018. *The Atlantic.*

37. Warren, Elizabeth. "A Foreign Policy For All." November 29, 2018. *Foreign Affairs.*

38. Farley, Robert. "Krugman Says Bush Was First President to Lead Country into War and Cut Taxes." November 30, 2009. *Politifact.*

39. "History of the US Income Tax (Business Reference Services)." Last Updated February 27, 2018. Library of Congress.

40. Cramer, Jim. "Sen. Elizabeth Warren On Trade Deals." August 15, 2018. *Mad Money.* CNBC.

41. "Trump's Own Economists Now Agree: GOP Tax Cuts Are Failing to Spark Growth." March 21, 2019. *Salon.*

42. Yglesias, Matt. "Elizabeth Warren Wants to Outflank Trump on Trade." November 29, 2018. *Vox.*

43. Toosi, Nahal, Gabby Orr, and Eliana Johnson. "A Moment of Crisis': Warren Lays Out Foreign Policy Vision." November 29, 2018. *Politico*.

44. "Check Out Senator Elizabeth Warren's Environmental Voting Record." League of Conservation Voters Scorecard. Accessed March 28, 2019.

45. "Vote on Undermining Flood Insurance Reform." 2019. League of Conservation Voters Scorecard. Accessed March 28, 2019.

46. Office of Senator Elizabeth Warren. "Warren, Colleagues Unveil Bill to Require Every Public Company to Disclose Climate-Related Risks." September 17, 2018. Warren.Senate.gov.

47. Republican Platform. "Restoring the American Dream." Accessed March 26, 2018. Republican National Committee.

48. Walden, Greg, Fred Upton, and John Shimkus. "Republicans Have Better Solutions to Climate Change." February 13, 2019. Realclearpolicy.com.

49. Office of Senator Elizabeth Warren. "Warren Introduces Accountable Capitalism Act." August 15, 2018. Warren.Senate.gov.

50. Bogle, John. "Opinion | The Supreme Court Had Its Say. Now Let Shareholders Decide." May 14, 2011. *New York Times*.

51. Office of Senator Elizabeth Warren. "Accountable Capitalism Act One-Pager." August 15, 2018. Warren.Senate.gov.

52. Office of Senator Elizabeth Warren. "STATES Act One-Pager" June 7, 2018. Warren.Senate.gov.

53. Bloomberg TV. "Senator Cory Gardner (R-CO) discusses his bill that would allow banking for the marijuana industry."

https://bloom.bg/2QSS7z5." Video. December 17, 2018, at 10:36 a.m. https://twitter.com/BloombergTV/status/1074689679813943296.

54. Martin, Naomi, and James Pindell. "Marijuana Legalization and the 2020 Presidential Race: Where the Candidates Stand." February 27, 2019. *Boston Globe*.

55. Masket, Seth. "Democrats Used to Disagree About Gun Control. the 2020 Candidates Don't." February 11, 2019. *Pacific Standard*.

56. Martin, Jonathan, and Abby Goodnough. "Medicare for All Emerges as Early Policy Test for 2020 Democrats." February 2, 2019. *New York Times*.

57. Uhrmacher, Kevin, Kevin Schaul, Paulina Firozi, and Jeff Stein. "Where 2020 Democrats stand on Medicare-for-all." March 15, 2019. *Washington Post*.

58. Stracqualursi, Veronica. "Sen. Warren: Replace ICE with 'Something That Reflects Our Morality.'" June 30, 2018. CNN.

59. ABC News Politics. "'I am angry on behalf of women who have been told to sit down and shut up.' Sen. Elizabeth Warren joins anti-Kavanaugh protesters in Washington, DC: 'I believe Dr. Ford. I watched that hearing last Thursday and Brett Kavanaugh is disqualified' http://abcn.ws/2O1B5xQ." Video. October 4, 2018, at 12:42 p.m. https://twitter.com/ABCPolitics/status/1047889774961352704.

CHAPTER 5

1. Chapel, Vondel, and Barbara Herring. "View Barbara Herring's Obituary On Newsok.com And Share Memories." August 20, 2007. *The Oklahoman*.

2. Elizabeth Warren For Massachusetts. "The Story of an American Family." Accessed March 24, 2019.

3. Ebbert, Stephanie. "Family Long a Bedrock for Warren | Boston .com." October 24, 2012. Boston.com.

4. Kreisler, Harry. "Conversation with Elizabeth Warren, P. 1 Of 4." March 8, 2007. Institute of International Studies, UC Berkeley.

5. Ivry, Bob, and Mark Pittman. "Warren Winning Means No Sale If You Can't Explain It (Update1)." November 19, 2009. Bloomberg News.

6. McGrane, Victoria. "Religion Is Constant Part of Elizabeth Warren's Life." September 2, 2017. *Boston Globe.*

7. Harvard Law School. "Elizabeth Warren | Harvard Law School Directory." Hls.Harvard.Edu. Accessed March 24, 2019.

8. Warren, Elizabeth. "My grandkids make me feel like the luckiest Gammy in the world. I was tickled to have them with me in Los Angeles last weekend!" Video. March 2, 2019. 5:43 p.m. https:// twitter.com/ewarren/status/1101976370412953603.

9. Halpern, Sue. "A Glimmer of Hope on the First Official Day of Elizabeth Warren's Presidential Campaign." February 10, 2019. *New Yorker.*

10. Packer, George. *The Unwinding: An Inner History of the New America.* 2014. New York: Farrar, Straus and Giroux.

CHAPTER 6

1. Curriculum Vitae. "Elizabeth Warren, Leo Gottlieb Professor of Law." Accessed March 22, 2019. http://www.law.harvard.edu/faculty/ewarren/Warren%20CV%20062508.pdf.

2. "Oversight of the Troubled Asset Relief Program." Wikipedia. https://en.wikipedia.org/wiki/Oversight_of_the_Troubled_Asset_Relief_Program#Congressional_Oversight_Panel_(COP). Accessed March 27, 2019.

3. The Commonwealth of Massachusetts. "[Voter] Enrollment Breakdown as of 10/17/2012." November 6, 2012.

4. Warren, Elizabeth, Jay Lawrence Westbrook, Katherine Porter, and John Pottow. *The Law of Debtors and Creditors: Text, Cases, And Problems*, seventh edition. August 19, 2014. Aspen Law School.

5. Schreckinger, Ben, Jack Shafer, and John Harris. "Why Elizabeth Warren Needs to Give 'The Speech.'" February 12, 2019. *Politico*.

6. See Chapter 3.

7. Warren, Elizabeth. *All Your Worth*. 2005. Free Press, New York, NY.

8. Hamm, Trent. "Review: All Your Worth—the Simple Dollar." May 11, 2007. *The Simple Dollar*. https://www.thesimpledollar.com/review-all-your-worth/.

9. Testimony of Elizabeth Warren, Leo Gottlieb Professor of Law Harvard Law School, Before the Committee on Banking, Housing, and Urban Affairs of the United States Senate Hearing: Examining the Billing, Marketing, and Disclosure Practices of the Credit Card Industry, and Their Impact on Consumers January 25, 2007.

Banking.Senate.gov. https://www.banking.senate.gov/imo/media/doc/warren.pdf.

10. Dealbook. "Panel Finds TARP Effective (Problems Aside)." December 9, 2009. *New York Times*.

11. Warren, Elizabeth. "Fighting To Protect Consumers." September 17, 2010. Whitehouse.gov. https://obamawhitehouse.archives.gov/blog/2010/09/17/fighting-protect-consumers.

12. "President Barack Obama, Treasury Secretary Timothy F. Geithner and Elizabeth Warren Walk Along the Colonnade." September 17, 2010. The White House.

13. "President Obama Names Elizabeth Warren Assistant to the President and Special Advisor to the Secretary of the Treasury on the Consumer Financial Protection Bureau." September 17, 2010. Whitehouse.gov.

14. Phillip, Abby. "Obama Taps Warren for Watchdog Job." September 17, 2010. *Politico*.

15. "2012 Massachusetts Senate: Brown Vs Warren–Polls–Huffpost Pollster." Accessed March 26, 2019. *Huffington Post*. https://elections.huffingtonpost.com/pollster/2012-massachusetts-senate-brown-vs-warren.

16. Madison, Lucy. "Elizabeth Warren: 'There Is Nobody in this Country Who Got Rich on His Own.'" September 22, 2011. CBS News.

17. Kiely, Eugene. "'You Didn't Build That,' Uncut And Unedited—Factcheck.org." July 23, 2012. Factcheck.org.

18. Sink, Justin. "Tough Scott Brown Ad Hits Warren on Obama's 'You Didn't Build That' Remark." July 23, 2012. *The Hill*.

19. Payne, Dan. "What's Wrong with the Warren Campaign." September 11, 2012. WBUR News, 90.9.

20. AP/Mass Live. "Elizabeth Warren's Native American Ancestry Claims Under Fire in US Senate Race." May 1, 2012. Masslive.com.

21. Franke-Ruta, Garance. "Elizabeth Warren: 'The System Is Rigged.'" September 6, 2012. *The Atlantic.*

22. Ibid.

23. Chozik, Amy. "'A Fighting Chance,' By Elizabeth Warren." April 26, 2014. *New York Times.*

CHAPTER 7

1. "Elizabeth Warren/Committees–Ballotpedia." Accessed March 26, 2019. Ballotpedia. https://ballotpedia.org/Elizabeth_Warren /Committees.

2. Bresnahan, John. "Reid Taps Warren as Envoy to Liberals." November 12, 2014. *Politico.*

3. Barrett, Ted, and Jeremy Diamond. 2019. "Elizabeth Warren Joins Senate Democratic Leadership." November 13, 2014. CNN.

4. Homans, Charles. "The New Party of No." March 13, 2017. *New York Times.*

5. "U.S. Senate: Leadership & Officers." Accessed March 23, 2019. Senate.gov. http://www.senate.gov/senators/leadership.htm.

6. Chappell, Bill. "'You Should Resign': Watch Sen. Elizabeth Warren Grill Wells Fargo CEO John Stumpf." September 20, 2016. NPR.

7. C-SPAN. @SenWarren #WellsFargo CEO: 'You should resign. You should give back the money that you took . . .'" Video. September 20, 2016, 12:14 p.m. https://twitter.com/cspan/status /778266130909499392.

8. Gonzales, Richard. "Wells Fargo CEO John Stumpf Resigns Amid Scandal." April 20, 2018. NPR.

9. "United States of America Bureau of Consumer Financial Protection Administrative Proceeding File No. 2018-BCFP-0001." April 20, 2018. Files.Consumerfinance.gov.

10. Fleishman, Glenn. "Elizabeth Warren Wants Wells Fargo Kicked Out of Colleges." January 17, 2019. *Fortune.*

11. Office of Senator Elizabeth Warren. "Warren Questions Wells Fargo CEO Tim Sloan on Excessively High Fees The Bank Charged College Students | U.S. Senator Elizabeth Warren of Massachusetts." January 17, 2019. Warren.Senate.gov.

12. "Senator Elizabeth Warren at Boston Logan Airport for #Nobannowall Protest." January 29, 2017. Youtube. https://www .youtube.com/watch?v=htAJKgt1KZs.

13. Kapur, Sahil. "Elizabeth Warren says a Sessions AG nom means Trump is 'embracing the bigotry that fueled his campaign rallies.'" Photo. November 18, 2016, 2:33 p.m. https://twitter.com/sahilkapur /status/799697128054353920.

14. "'Nevertheless, She Persisted': How Senate's Silencing of Warren Became a Meme." February 8, 2017. *New York Times.*

15. Harris, Kamala. "By silencing Elizabeth Warren, the GOP gave women around the world a rallying cry. #ShePersisted

#LetLizSpeak." Photo. February 8, 2019, 12:19 p.m. https://twitter
.com/KamalaHarris/status/829379045729169410.

16. Office of Senator Elizabeth Warren. Congress Passes "Smart Savings
Act" to Strengthen Retirement Savings for Federal Employees | U.S.
Senator Elizabeth Warren of Massachusetts." December 15, 2014.
Warren.Senate.gov.

17. "Massachusetts Medical Society: Mass. Medical Society
Applauds Passage of 'Partial Fill' Legislation." July 14, 2016.
Massmed.org.

18. Office of Senator Elizabeth Warren. "Bipartisan Over-The-Counter
Hearing Aid Legislation to Become Law | U.S. Senator Elizabeth
Warren of Massachusetts." August 3, 2017. Warren.Senate.gov.

19. Rifkin, Jesse. "Almost Unanimous, 2017 Edition: We Asked Why
These Lone Dissenters Withheld Their Votes on Bills." October 9,
2016. *Medium*. Govtrack Insider.

20. Kiger, Patrick. "Senate Votes to Allow OTC Hearing Aids." August
4, 2017. AARP.

21. Karlin-Smith, Sarah, and Rachael Bade. "Senate Approves 'Right-To-
Try' Drug Bill." August 3, 2017. *Politico*.

22. "S.1393 - 115th Congress (2017–2018): Jobs for Our Heroes Act."
January 8, 2018. Congress.gov.

23. Brooks, Drew. "Bill Easing CDL Requirements for Veterans
Becomes Law." January 13, 2018. *Fayetteville Observer*.

24. "Cornyn, Warren Introduce Bill to Prevent 'Forum-Shopping' in
Bankruptcy Cases." January 8, 2018. United States Senator John
Cornyn, Texas.

25. See Chapter 4.

26. "Elizabeth Warren, Senator For Massachusetts - Govtrack.us Analysis." Accessed March 27, 2019. Govtrack.us. https://www.govtrack.us/congress/members/elizabeth_warren/412542.

27. "Elizabeth Warren's 2018 Legislative Statistics." Accessed March 27, 2019. Govtrack.us. https://www.govtrack.us/congress/members/elizabeth_warren/412542/report-card/2018.

28. Caban, Antonio. "Geoff Diehl Says He Was Co-Chair of Trump's Bay State Campaign. Was He?" October 31, 2018. WGBH.

29. AP News. "BREAKING: Democrat Elizabeth Warren wins re-election to U.S. Senate from Massachusetts. #APracecall at 8:00 p.m. EST. @AP election coverage: http://apne.ws/APPolitics #Election2018 #MAelection." November 6, 2018, 8:01 p.m. https://twitter.com/AP_Politics/status/1059974083591462915.

30. "2018 United States Senate Election in Massachusetts." Accessed March 22, 2019. En.Wikipedia.org.

31. DeCosta-Klipa, Nick. "Elizabeth Warren's Re-Election Victory Speech: Read the Full Transcript | Boston.com." November 7, 2018. Boston.com.

32. Buell, Spencer. "Elizabeth Warren Wins. She's Still Your Senator, for Now." November 6, 2018. *Boston* Magazine.

33. Freedlander, David. "Obama's 2008 Backers: We're Ready for Warren." October 9, 2014. *The Daily Beast*. https://www.thedailybeast.com/obamas-2008-backers-were-ready-for-warren.

34. Disclosure: Series editor Scott Dworkin's company was hired by the Ready for Warren PAC as a political adviser in 2014.

35. McGrane, Victoria. "Five Things To Know About Elizabeth Warren's Record In The US Senate." November 2, 2018. *Boston Globe*.

CHAPTER 8

1. Steve Peoples, Elana Schor and Hunter Woodall. "Warren Embraces Underdog Role as She Faces 2020 Challenges." March 18, 2019. AP NEWS.

2. Ingraham, Christopher. "Over 60 Percent of Voters—Including Half of Republicans—Support Elizabeth Warren's Wealth Tax." February 5, 2019. *Washington Post*.

3. Hughes, Greg, and John King. "Elizabeth Warren's Polling Problem: Gaining Support From Next Door." March 3, 2019. CNN.

4. "Realclearpolitics–Election 2020–New Hampshire Democratic Presidential Primary." Accessed March 30, 2019. Realclearpolitics .com.

5. "Emerson Polling—Iowa 2020: Biden and Sanders Neck and Neck in Democratic Field, Mayor Pete Jumps to Double Digits." March 24, 2019. Emersonpolling.Reportablenews.com. https:// emersonpolling.reportablenews.com/pr/iowa-2020-biden-and -sanders-neck-and-neck-in-democratic-field-mayor-pete-jumps-to -double-digits.

6. "Emerson Polling—Wisconsin 2020: Bernie Sanders Leads Democratic Field; Trump Competitive in General Election." March 17, 2019. Emersonpolling.Reportablenews.com. https://emersonpoll-ing.reportablenews.com/pr/wisconsin-2020-bernie-sanders-leads -democratic-field-trump-competitive-in-general-election.

7. "Fox News Poll 3/24/2019." March 24, 2019. Foxnews.com. https://www.foxnews.com/politics/fox-news-poll-3-24-2019.

8. Vesoulis, Abby, and Philip Elliott. "Elizabeth Warren Bucks the Trend by Running on Ideas." March 22, 2019. *Time* magazine.